DECORATING A ROOM OF ONE'S OWN

For everyone who loves books and homes

and homes in books

DECORATING A ROOM OF ONE'S OWN

CONVERSATIONS ON INTERIOR DESIGN WITH
MISS HAVISHAM, JANE EYRE, VICTOR FRANKENSTEIN,
ELIZABETH BENNET, ISHMAEL, AND
OTHER LITERARY NOTABLES

BY SUSAN HARLAN
ILLUSTRATIONS BY BECCA STADTLANDER

ABRAMS IMAGE, NEW YORK

CONTENTS

INTRODUCTION

THE IDEA FOR THIS BOOK came to me one evening while I was doing something that I am often doing: sitting on my couch with my dog, Millie, watching a movie and drinking a Manhattan. On this particular evening, I was watching the 1997 *Jane Eyre* starring Samantha Morton and Ciarán Hinds. This is only one of several *Jane Eyre* adaptations that I return to again and again rather than actually watching anything new. It was February and cold and gloomy outside—perfect *Jane Eyre* weather. How could I watch anything else?

Like other *Jane Eyre* films, this one features a great Thornfield Hall. The exterior is Naworth Castle in Cumbria, and the interior is Knebworth House in Hertfordshire. This composite Thornfield is gloomy, dark, and Gothic in the extreme, as it should be. As I watched Morton's Jane Eyre adjust to her new surroundings, another interest of mine popped into my head: the world of home decorating and design. I started to notice things like the candlesticks, the chairs, and the rugs. The art on the walls. The fireplace and the mantel. *I wouldn't mind a rug like that*, I thought. *All nice and worn down.* And so Thornfield Hall became an accidental decorating inspiration, an idea that struck me as darkly funny, given the tragedies and horrors that the house holds. I grabbed my laptop and started to take notes while I watched the movie. What if Jane were interested in paint colors and cushions? Maybe scorched-by-a-fire-set-by-your-husband's-doomed-secret-wife is the new shabby chic.

I was no stranger to the world of home-design sites and blogs, as my house had been featured as an *Apartment Therapy* House Tour a year earlier. I had lived in the small city of Winston-Salem, North Carolina for about four years, first renting a unit in a larger house and then moving into a duplex. I moved out of the duplex in 2012 to undertake a one-year research sabbatical, which took me to New York City, Washington, DC, and Pasadena, and when I came back through town on my drive from New York to California, I spotted a house for sale in the same old, historic neighborhood I had lived in before. It was quite cute. It was also cheap. I hadn't thought about buying a house, but no one had made an offer on this one, perhaps because it needed some work—really just a fresh coat of paint and some landscaping. It was a 1920s shingled house, two stories and two thousand square feet: quite luxurious for one person and her pooch. So I bought it. And named her Maud because she was an old dame. And then I got to work settling in. I had loved decorating my other places in Winston-Salem, as well as my prewar, fourth-floor walk-up apartment in Morningside Heights in New York City, where I had lived during graduate school, but now I could do things like *paint the walls*. Even paint them dark colors. This was too exciting for words. When everything was in order, I submitted it to *Apartment Therapy*, and a writer named Tamara Gavin came from Asheville to interview me and take pictures. We talked about the house and had barbecue for lunch. It was a lot of fun.

Once I had written my Jane Eyre "House Tour," I knew where I wanted to send it: the Toast. I had written a few essays for the site and admired its combination of wit and intelligence. My editor, Nicole Chung, liked the idea and accepted it, and *Great House Therapy* was born. I was fortunate to write for the Toast as the site succeeded in doing something almost unheard of on the Internet, particularly for women writers who are accustomed to online harassment: It created a supportive and vibrant community of writers and readers. When I started writing non-academically several years ago, I was told by writer friends *never* to read the comments.

In general, I've been pretty good about this, and when I'm tempted, a quick glance is enough to remind me of the wisdom of this advice. The Toast is the only site I have written for where not only did I read the comments, I *looked forward* to reading the comments. It was a genuine pleasure to go through readers' posts. Being an English professor can be an isolating job. I was happy for the sense of camaraderie that I found with the Toast. Now the Toast is no more, but its spirit remains. Even as I write this, I find that I'm smiling.

I wrote eight more columns for Nicole, choosing novels and plays that I often taught at Wake Forest University and others that I just thought would be a kick. Still others were childhood classics that I wanted to revisit. These homes tell us about characters. They tell us about communities. And they tell us about the past. You can't think about *Pride and Prejudice* without thinking about Pemberley. In fact, Elizabeth can't think about Darcy without it; she falls in love with him when she sees his house. From the landscape in which it is set to its interior—and the portrait of Darcy that she admires—Pemberley reveals the real Darcy, not the version of the town's gossip or even the version that Darcy himself (badly) performs. When I teach *Hamlet*, we always talk about Elsinore. Shakespeare's stage has been called a "bare stage." The outdoor London amphitheaters where his plays were often performed did not have sets—or not what we think of as sets today. The audience had to imagine Elsinore, as the chorus of *Henry V* asked them to imagine the horses and armies of the battle of Agincourt at the beginning of that play. These things could not be presented; they had to be conjured. Elsinore is the place to which the ghost of King Hamlet returns. It is the place where Ophelia is buried. It is the place where Hamlet and Laertes engage in a fencing match to entertain the court. It is a place of surveillance: Everyone is watching everyone else. It has a character all its own. It is an entrapping place. Ensnaring. Corrupt. Dangerous. Rotten.

But in working on this book, I also had the opportunity to explore literary homes that were less familiar. This was particularly true of the classics that I hadn't reread since I was a younger: books like *Anne of Green Gables*, *The Swiss Family Robinson*, and *Pippi Longstocking*. *Anne of Green Gables* still has the power to charm. Along with *Little Women*, it will always be one of the books that made me want to be bookish. To teach. To write. Other classics have aged less well. *Pippi Longstocking*, which I remember as an incredible fantasy of childhood independence (who needs parents?), is a racist disaster. And then of course there is always the question of gender, particularly when you're writing about homes, which have traditionally been a female domain. When I watched the 1960 Disney film *Swiss Family Robinson* as a kid, the tree house made quite an impression. I wanted that tree house. In the book, the house is the mother's idea, and the father is resistant; she has to convince him that her plan will work. But in the film, the house is the father's idea—a surprise for his wife—and she is so overwhelmed by his generosity that she professes she does not deserve it. The film is a glossy, terrifying reimagining of the book: The hardworking husband provides for his beautiful, good, passive wife, even on a deserted island. The décor has a distinctly mid-century vibe, and he even builds a dream kitchen, just like those spaces back home where suburban wives whiled away the hours after World War II. There is an icebox that is clearly a refrigerator: not something Johann David Wyss had in mind in 1812. It is fun to mock the sexism of some classics; it feels like resistance. And some books are so over-the-top that they already seem like satire. That was my sense in revisiting *Great Expectations*. Miss Havisham is affecting and terribly sad, but she's also an undeniable cocktail of misogynist clichés. It's hard to take a moldy wedding cake seriously. Or all the cobwebs. Mocking these things seems like the only reasonable response.

I find literary homes fascinating as an English professor, but I also find them fascinating personally. They make me see my own home differently, and they remind me that ideas of home are always shifting. Some homes are stable and unchanging. Some are dynamic. My home is the latter. She is constantly changing; one of my decorating models is Auntie Mame. It has been four years since my *Apartment Therapy* House Tour, and if my house seemed finished (or full) then, it certainly was not. I'm always adding another odd work of art (I'm a big fan of vintage Paint by Number paintings), fridge magnet, quilt, chair, dish, or paperweight. Or my taxidermy parakeet named Priscilla. I spend a lot of time searching for treasures at flea markets and antiques malls, both in my current home of Winston-Salem and on the many road trips I take through the South, so the things in my house remind me of my travels. I like to bring the world back to Maud.

I have undertaken a couple of home improvement projects. When I moved into the house, there was a kitchen upstairs; for the former owner, the house had been sort of a duplex. I had the kitchen torn out and turned into a guest room, and then I had the pleasure of decorating a new room. I painted the walls a peacock green I think Phryne Fisher would like. I also added a cabinet of curiosities in a strange nook off the dining room. Like a Renaissance *Wunderkammer*, it is filled with shells, rocks, plants, feathers, butterflies, bones, and fossils. An ostrich egg. A grave rubbing from a cemetery in a small town in Texas. A plastic skeleton named John Donne from a Halloween store. Since my *Apartment Therapy* House Tour focused on how my house was already a cabinet of curiosities, it seemed like a sensible next step to actually put one together. I also bought myself a taxidermy mule deer named Wentworth (who is unquestionably the most romantic Austen hero). He is too large for the cabinet of curiosities, so he hangs in the living room, presiding over everything like a household god.

Some things from my house, and from my life, appear in the House Tours here. Heidi's preference for the style of mock-Bavarian villages was inspired by a trip to Helen, Georgia, where I stayed in the Heidi Motel. The book also includes three great gifts I received for my fortieth birthday in 2017: a Jonathan Adler Paris throw pillow, a print of Warhol's *Dolly Parton*, and a commissioned portrait of my dog, Millie. And writing this book changed my own surroundings. I have always liked to keep my books in stacks on the floor. It's true that it can be hard to get to one on the bottom, but in general, having them all right there makes me feel as though I can just grab anything. There is an appealing immediacy to a book stack. And your books feel so connected to your home, there on the floor, at ease. Sometimes I pick up a book and reread it just because it is on top of one of the stacks. Sometimes I put the prettiest covers on the top. I had a number of these book towers in my foyer, arranged around a large antique radio, but over the past few years they had expanded into the adjacent sitting room as well. I found that the books around the radio were three stacks deep, and for the first time, I had to think about cutting them back if I wanted to be able to find anything while writing this book. Where was *Bleak House*? Where was *To Kill a Mockingbird*? Or *Dracula*? Did I have a copy of *Rebecca*? I realized that although I loved my book stacks, they were proliferating and posing some practical problems.

Over the course of a few weeks, I put my books in order. I divided everything by genre, grouping some books by author or time period, and I had six bookshelves installed, high on the walls (the only wall space left in my place). Three were quite long—about ten feet each—and the three were four feet, so I was able to get a number of my volumes off the floor and in place. I also acquired a number of books in writing this, sometimes because I couldn't find my copy and sometimes because I decided I needed a beautiful new edition. I bought six of the Puffin Penguin Pantone editions of children's classics. And I acquired a few new editions designed by Coralie Bickford-Smith, including *Twenty Thousand Leagues Under the Sea*, *Robinson Crusoe*, *Frankenstein*, and *The Picture of Dorian Gray*. So as I sat on my front porch, reading about imagined houses, I was reading editions that also make my house beautiful. There is a kind of ceremony to reading a lovely book, and when you are finished, you get to look at it, there in your home, and one day you will take it off the shelf and read it again. Now I have about thirty of these Bickford-Smith classics, lined up in a colorful row on a shelf in my living room. As I write this, I still have thirty-five feet of books to shelve, but I'm enjoying the process. My bookshelves make me think about writing this book; they are the result of this book, and vice-versa. And when I need *Frankenstein,* I know where it is. I still have six good stacks on the floor, so my love of stacks is safe.

My house is a place to think and read and have long conversations with friends and hang out with my dog and write. In the end, decorating a house is a lot like writing. You are arranging things in relationship to other things in a precise and thoughtful way in order to create something beautiful. You are choosing to surround yourself with significant things, and you are choosing to live in a realm that is significant—a realm that means something to you—and you are the one who determines what matters.

I.

ANCESTRAL ESTATES

(REAL AND FAKE)

Jane Austen, Pride and Prejudice

ELIZABETH AND DARCY'S
NEITHER FORMAL NOR FALSELY ADORNED
PAD OF PRIVILEGE

Names: Elizabeth, feisty heroine who nonetheless fully conforms to patriarchal expectations, and Darcy, reformed grouch and scantily clad swimmer in lakes

Location: Derbyshire, England

Size: Bigger and better than all other houses in the county (ask anyone)

Years lived in: Since Darcy was the sweetest-tempered, most generous-hearted boy in the world; owned

O NE YEAR AGO, after their lavish boho-chic wedding to which all the county was invited, Elizabeth moved into Darcy's family seat of Pemberley. Their home, which is located in one of the hippest and most desired neighborhoods in England, dates so far back that no one would dare question its authenticity and awesomeness.

Their shared love of fountains and ease with their social position shine through in many details of this extraordinary home. Darcy and Elizabeth live with Darcy's sister, Georgiana, and their staff, which includes the devoted housekeeper, Mrs. Reynolds, whom Darcy warmly describes as "sort of like my mother, but not, of course, because she's a servant." Although the house is perfect, they hope to make some improvements. They anticipate converting several of the bedrooms into nurseries in the coming years, where nursemaids will strive to keep the little ones out of sight until they are sent to school. Both are hoping for a boy, as girls are utterly useless in a system of primogeniture.

It was important to Elizabeth to put her stamp on Pemberley when she took up residence, so she visited some other lovely, but duly inferior, estates like Chatsworth for inspiration. With its 126 rooms and extensive gardens, Chatsworth is "not at all bad," she says, but Darcy insists that it is "utter garbage" compared to Pemberley, which has a much better point of view, situated as it is on the opposite side of a valley into which the road with some abruptness winds.

The Darcys like large, well-proportioned rooms that are handsomely fitted up, and Darcy himself likes to take baths. Elizabeth enjoys long walks in the woods, from which she returns with flushed cheeks that are obviously totally sexual.

All in all, they have created a home of seven thousand rooms where they can welcome Elizabeth's family, although they desperately hope that those fools will not visit too often. Elizabeth allowed us a peek into the beauties of Pemberley.

A CHAT WITH ELIZABETH

THEIR STYLE

I would describe our style as neither gaudy nor uselessly fine, by which I mean it's not disgusting like Rosings, which looks like somebody vomited up chintz and then covered everything that didn't move in gold. Lady Catherine de Bourgh showed up right after I moved in and wanted to tell me how to decorate, but I told her I'd rather be stuck on a desert island with my idiot sisters than listen to her nonsense. She backed off after that, and I haven't seen her beady little judgmental eyes in some time. Truth be told, I don't think Darcy would want me interfering too much in the material manifestation of his masculine, masterly virtue, but I do make

the occasional tweak: a new Ming vase here, an embalmed pygmy person there. We have a lot of Greek statues, and of course the portraits of Darcy in the picture gallery. I know it may sound narcissistic to have a lot of paintings of oneself, but it's just something you do if you're important. My favorite is the one where he's standing over the bleeding body of a defenseless fox.

INSPIRATION

In making a few changes to some of the parlors, I was influenced by design elements of my former home, Longbourn, where I always had to listen to my idiot sisters fighting over bonnets. I really loved my father's library. I was enamored of the mahogany bookshelves, his beautiful desk set, and his charmingly worn leather club chair. He really made a gorgeous room into which he could retreat from all of us. It's funny that I should think of this, because now I'm seeing a psychoanalyst and working through some issues I have about how he talked down to my mother, his total disregard for all our welfare, and, well—a few things. My analyst, Prunella, says that one's relationship to one's father is very important. I'm going to start going five times a week.

FAVORITE ELEMENT

The situation of the house and the extensive gardens. This was what made me first fall in love with the place—I mean, with Darcy! Sorry. My, oh my. Seeing the house really put my spirits in a high flutter, and my mind was too full for conversation, but I saw and admired every remarkable spot and point of view. It was a large, handsome stone building, standing well on rising ground, and backed by a ridge of high woody hills. In front, a stream of some natural importance was swelled into greater, but without any artificial appearance. I was delighted. But you know the deal—this is all detailed at the beginning of chapter 43. Now that I'm recalling this moment, it's almost as if this description has larger implications for understanding the social position and values of the landed gentry in England. I'll have to think about that later, when I'm filling the endless hours of my day.

WHAT FRIENDS SAY

Jane and Bingley like Pemberley a lot, probably because it's bigger than their place. I mean, Netherfield Park is great, if you're into smaller, cozier rooms. They come to hang out and to remind us how much nicer they are than us. But Darcy and I are also homebodies, and we just like to enjoy the space. He still finds country society somewhat confined and unvarying for his taste, so he often stays in and cleans his guns while I go out to dance mechanically in rows. And we throw parties regularly, although my idiot sisters aren't allowed to drink or play the piano.

WHAT THE SERVANTS SAY

There have been some growing pains. Sometimes our housekeeper, Mrs. Reynolds, forgets to dust certain parlors or to change the flowers in the bedrooms on the eighth floor, but that's probably because we never told her those rooms were there. Darcy is the best landlord and the best master—not to mention the handsomest. Just the other day, he gave our groom a half-day off because his father is dying in another county, so that was nice. All our servants are thrilled to work at Pemberley. Sometimes I wonder if they might have wanted to do something different with their lives, but then I think: Crazy lady, they love it!

BIGGEST EMBARRASSMENT

A lack of closet space, definitely! We have a lot of clothes, and of course there are Darcy's guns, and it's hard to know where to put everything. I've purchased a few lovely wardrobes from Paris, and that has made a difference. But honestly, the lack of closet space is a real downside of a Great House that no one tells you about when you're a young heroine looking for a single man in possession of a good fortune. I'm hoping to install some California Closets when things calm down after the hunting season.

PROUDEST DIY

Well, Caroline Bingley came to visit a few days ago, and I needlepointed her head to a pillow. HA! Just kidding. It's a truth universally acknowledged that an armchair in possession of a large bottom must be in want of a throw pillow, so I have made a few new pillows for the south drawing room, although I haven't been over to that part of the house in several weeks. I also burned the portrait of George Wickham. Does that count as a DIY project? I did make the fire. I think he might have noticed its absence the last time he and Lydia were here, but maybe not since he was drunk the whole time.

BIGGEST INDULGENCE

We like to buy books for our library, and I have a lot of time to read as I lack an active and useful profession. At first, I was a bit uncomfortable in the space as it brings to mind my issues with my father's library, but I'm coming to like it. I also bought myself a nice writing desk. It's from China, where the opium comes from. I fill my days by writing letters, making sure Mrs. Reynolds has her orders, and helping Darcy's younger sister, Georgiana, learn how to speak words out loud. I have bought a few lovely things and sent them to my best friend, Charlotte, but she doesn't really visit anymore. I suppose I could bring that up with my analyst next week.

BEST ADVICE

Give a lot of balls, but don't invite officers! Sketchy guys, the lot. As I said, Wickham and Lydia came to visit recently, and of course they didn't even bring a bottle of wine. Wickham mostly played billiards with himself and kept requesting that servant girls come to his room to fix some issue with the fire. But yes, the balls have been fun, and they have given me something to do. Being mistress of Pemberley really is something, but it's not all claret and roses. Let's see. What else? I also suggest that you design yourself a work-life-balance studio. I did, and I can't tell you how great it's been. I redecorated one of our seven thousand rooms in a lovely shade of green that reminds me of my long walks in the countryside, and until that decorating moment, I never knew myself.

HOW TO DECORATE LIKE A GENTLEMAN WITH MR. KNIGHTLEY

"I own most of Highbury, but this responsibility doesn't keep me from focusing on important details at my home, Donwell Abbey. An abbey is such a delight. I'm so fortunate that the dissolution of the monasteries during the Reformation made all this real estate available. But if you also own an abbey, don't feel obligated to adopt an overly monastic style. That would be badly done indeed! Take inspiration from other estates that you visit regularly and maybe even don't own. Think about what works and what doesn't. For example, Hartfield is rather claustrophobic. So don't allow fearful old men to dictate style. And make your décor work for you. But really, make everyone work for you because that's what you do when everything belongs to you."

Emily Brontë, Wuthering Heights

CATHY AND HEATHCLIFF'S GHOST-INFESTED RESIDENCE OF REVENGE AND REGRET

Name: Ellen "Nelly" Dean, housekeeper and provider of a tremendous amount of unrewarded and unacknowledged female emotional labor (more about Cathy and Heathcliff to come)

Location: Yorkshire, near Gimmerton

Size: Quite large and imposing, with many buildings

Years lived in: Since forever; owned by Cathy's father, then by her brother, Hindley, and eventually acquired by Heathcliff in an anger-fueled real estate transaction

SOME HOMES ARE DEFINED by the warm and wonderful memories they hold. Wuthering Heights is not one of those homes, but it is suited to brooding, illness, unfortunate life choices, and psychological delusions.

"We have some lovely griffin carvings," says Nelly.

"Wuthering" means exposed and storm blown; it is descriptive of the atmospheric tumult to which the home's station is exposed in stormy weather. Pure, bracing ventilation they must have up there at all times indeed. One may guess the power of the north wind blowing over the edge by the excessive slant of a few stunted firs at the end of the house and by a range of gaunt thorns all stretching their limbs one way, as if craving alms of the sun. Anyway. You get the general idea.

The inclement weather suits not only this dark and unsightly sixteenth-century farmhouse but also the identity-obliterating, pseudo-incestuous love between Cathy and Heathcliff for which the house is known.

"Those kids wore me out," she says. "Heathcliff even had a Cathy-related issue with the *kitchen floor*, if you can believe that. He said, 'What is not connected with her to me? And what does not recall her? I cannot look down to this floor, but her features are shaped in the flags!' I can't be expected to pick out a new floor because of his soul-destroying love. I have meat pies to make."

The house is filled with surprises, from a ghost's dead fingers tapping on windows to the occasional drunk and ruined man wandering its halls, muttering about his problems with his father. There is also Joseph, but no one understands him.

Wuthering Heights boasts embellished doorways, latticed windows, arched thresholds, and grotesque carvings around the main door, and it is lit by mood-setting candlelight that suggests Gothic visions of doom. Its inhabitants like eccentric antique finds and rustic contemporary pieces.

"I'm particularly fond of large pewter dishes, silver jugs, tankards, and dispensing advice to people who do not listen to me," Nelly says.

Neighboring Thrushcross Grange isn't too far away, where the boring Lintons live. It lies within a large park and has a nice parlor, a drawing room, and a garden.

"They also have a library over there, but they mostly just sit around and play cards and look at the walls," she says. "They're not the most riveting bunch, but they do like chandeliers."

A CHAT WITH NELLY

THEIR STYLE

Spare. Dark. Old horse pistols can liven up an otherwise drab wall. And we like canisters. I always say you can never have too many canisters. Cathy did, too. She would always say, "My love for bowls is like the foliage in the woods: time will change it, I'm well aware, as winter changes the trees. My love for canisters resembles the eternal rocks beneath: a source of little visible delight, but necessary." I mean, I'd like to see anyone bake a decent loaf of bread without a canister or two.

INSPIRATION

The kitchen inspires the design aesthetic of the entire home. You can never go wrong with a good, sturdy farmhouse table—something you can chop vegetables on and watch the moths fluttering among the heath and harebells and listen to the soft wind breathing through the grass and wonder how anyone could ever imagine unquiet slumbers for the sleepers in that quiet earth. If you can't find an authentic farmhouse table, CB2 has some good fake options.

IMPORTANT INFLUENCES

The headstones you see around here were an influence. I like that particular shade of gray. There's something simple and pared down about it. Like death, I suppose. And I'm quite influenced by the landscape of the moors. Sometimes I gather heath and moss and arrange it in an antique Ball jar. If I'm feeling crazy, I'll throw in a branch or two—the ones that are always scratching at the windows with the intense horror of a nightmare. Decorating is always in my mind: not as a pleasure, any more than I am always a pleasure to myself, but as my own being.

FAVORITE ELEMENT

Heathcliff's bedroom is quite a showstopper. There is a good carpet in there, which is obliterated by dust, several damaged chairs, deep indentations in the panels of the walls, and a fireplace hung with cut paper, dropping to pieces. The handsome oak bedstead with ample crimson curtains of rather expensive material and modern make is charming, if a bit overbearing and masculine. But that was Heathcliff!

WHAT FRIENDS SAY

Mr. Lockwood says, "Don't stop here, even if you are exhausted. Seriously. Stop absolutely anywhere else."

BIGGEST EMBARRASSMENT

Definitely Cathy's ghost. Or when Heathcliff dug up her body in a grief-fueled, maniacal fantasy of enduring love. That was gross. But the ghost is the real issue. It has a child's face and little, ice-cold hands and cries out that it is lost on the moor. "I've been a waif for twenty years!" it says. Well, we all have our problems. One guest dragged the little ghost's wrist on the broken windowpane, rubbing it to and fro till the blood ran down and soaked the bedclothes. And those were actually really nice bedclothes. Garnet Hill, I think. Not even on sale.

PROUDEST DIY

The bed in Heathcliff's room is carved with *Catherine Earnshaw, Catherine Heathcliff*, and *Catherine Linton*. It was thoughtless to just mark up the paint like this, without a sense of whether it would complement the style of the room. But compared to the ghost, I suppose it's not that big of a deal.

I got a new bench recently. It was a real splurge as I had just bought a new ladder, too.

PLANS FOR THE FUTURE

I'm thinking of listing the place on Airbnb as we have heard that city people find farmhouses "super charming," but we worry that Cathy's ghost might lead to negative reviews. But maybe we could list "Haunting Spirit" under "Amenities."

BEST ADVICE

Try to forgive people. The alternative is pretty dismal. And never pass up a deal on solid crockery in neutral colors.

LOVING YOUR HOME WITH
THE TENANT OF WILDFELL HALL

"Wildfell Hall is a superannuated mansion of the Elizabethan era built of dark gray stone—venerable and picturesque to look at, but, doubtless, cold and gloomy enough to inhabit, with its thick stone mullions and little latticed panes, its time-eaten airholes, and its too lonely, too unsheltered situation. Suffice to say that it needed serious work when my son and I arrived after fleeing my abusive and alcoholic husband. The place is more comfortable now as I wrought some changes in it—just repaired some broken windows and fixed the dilapidated roof. I doubt I'll do much more as no one really sees the place. I suppose I could invite some of my asshole neighbors over. But I wouldn't want to cut into the time they spend gossiping about me."

Charles Dickens, Bleak House

LEICESTER AND HONORIA'S
RAIN-SOAKED PLACE IN LINCOLNSHIRE

Names: Lady Honoria Dedlock, who possesses an exhausted composure, a worn-out placidity, and an equanimity of fatigue not to be ruffled by interest or satisfaction (also: She is at the center of the fashionable intelligence and at the top of the fashionable tree), and husband, Sir Leicester, haughty baronet extraordinaire

Location: Lincolnshire, England

Size: Sufficiently large to hide many secrets

Years lived in: A long time as Sir Leicester's family is as old as the hills and infinitely more respectable; owned

CHESNEY WOLD is everything one could hope for in an ancestral estate: It is picturesque and old, in a fine park, richly wooded. The house, with gable and chimney, and tower, and turret, and dark doorway, and broad terrace-walk, seems scarcely real in its light solidity. It even has a general smell and taste of the ancient Dedlocks in their graves, which is not the sort of thing you can fix with Febreze.

Sir Leicester is only a baronet, but there is no mightier baronet than he. He is ceremonious, stately, and most polite, as well as extremely gouty. As a young woman, Honoria (who is childless) possessed beauty, pride, ambition, insolent resolve, and sense enough to portion out a legion of fine ladies. Today, she resembles a sad but still attractive piece of dried-up toast and does very little apart from sitting in the long drawing room and reflecting on how bored she is.

An honorable, obstinate, truthful, high-spirited, intensely prejudiced, perfectly unreasonable man, Sir Leicester spends his days eating wild game and being gallant to his wife. In spite of her lowness of spirits, Honoria still finds the energy to occasionally stare out of windows. Her favorite window is the one in her boudoir. In the early twilight, she looks out at a keeper's lodge and sees the light of a fire upon the latticed panes, and smoke rising from the chimney, and a child, chased by a woman, running out into the rain to meet the shining figure of a wrapped-up man coming through the gate.

"I think it must be easier, and probably quite charming, to be poor," she says.

The view from her windows is alternately a lead-colored view and a view in Indian ink. The property is also known for its moldy little church, as well as a hell of a lot of animals—crows, rabbits, deer, partridges, pheasants, dogs, geese, and turkeys—that seem only to underscore the elegant lifelessness of the house itself.

"It is a deadened world, and its growth is sometimes unhealthy for want of air," she says. "I try to harness this sense of airlessness in my décor. Sometimes that means an ice sculpture that lends a freezing mood to a room. Or sometimes it means just closing up all the shutters and sitting in the dark for an afternoon."

And they simply could not do without their rather deaf housekeeper, Mrs. Rouncewell, who sits in her room (in a side passage on the ground floor, with an arched window commanding a smooth quadrangle, adorned at regular intervals with smooth round trees and smooth round blocks of stone, as if the trees were going to play at bowls with the stones), and the whole house reposes on her mind. So long as this iron-bosomed woman is taking care of everything, Sir Leicester and Honoria are free to travel to Paris or to simply lounge around and pick up cushions and then put them down again.

"I'd like to get that Jonathan Adler Paris needlepoint pillow—the one with the kissy lips and the Eiffel Tower—to remind me that I'm almost happy when I leave this place," Honoria says.

When moments of acute distress strike Honoria and send her careening back into the transgressions of her youth, she enjoys taking walks on the property.

"My husband would on the whole admit that Nature is a good idea (a little low, when not enclosed with a park fence), but an idea dependent for its execution on your great country families," she says. "I, on the other hand, would say that I don't really care one way or another. I just can't take the detestable monotony. It's enough to make you spontaneously combust."

A CHAT WITH LADY DEDLOCK

HER STYLE

I like candlesticks, things that are made of plaster, and tassels. I suppose. I am in very low spirits today.

HER INSPIRATION

Rockingham Castle. It has some very nice trees and shadows. I'm fond of trees and shadows, especially shadows. And rain is a big inspiration. It rains here nonstop. The vases on the stone terrace catch the rain all day; and the heavy drops fall, *drip, drip, drip,* upon the broad flagged pavement, called from old time the Ghost's Walk, all night. The horses get very miffed. I think we are seriously in some sort of strange weather pattern here.

IMPORTANT INFLUENCES

The color gray. Chesney Wold is extremely dreary, which suits me just fine. We also have a place in town, of course. But London is really foggy. Fog everywhere. Fog up the river, where it flows among green aits and meadows; fog down the river, where it rolls defiled among the tiers of shipping and the waterside pollutions of a great (and dirty) city. Fog on the Essex Marshes, fog on the Kentish heights. Fog creeping into the cabooses of collier brigs; fog lying out in the yards, and hovering in the rigging of great ships; fog drooping on the gunwales of barges and small boats. Fog in the eyes and throats of ancient Greenwich pensioners—god, I'm sorry to talk so much about the weather. I don't know what's wrong with me.

FAVORITE ELEMENT

The Ghost's Walk, which is not really a terrace where you would host a summer cocktail party so much as a place that is cursed. It is *so* well suited to this old echoing place. After all, only a family of such antiquity and importance has a right to a ghost. It's a family anecdote about an ancestor—Sir Morbury and his Lady—who led a troubled life. It is said that she had relations among King Charles's enemies, and a favorite brother of hers was killed in the civil wars, and she hated the race into which she had married, so she snuck into the stables at night and lamed the horses, and some other things that I won't go into because I'm already boring myself. The story is about hearing footsteps. You don't want that. That would be bad. If there are footsteps, there will be disgrace on the house of Dedlock. Because of the footsteps. And the horse laming and all that.

UNIQUE ELEMENT

My lady's maid, Rosa. I'm training her now. She's very innocent and beautiful and makes me feel like I could be innocent and beautiful again, too, and she also does my hair. She's very dedicated to me. Servants love to be servants. That's why they're always singing songs about it, like in *Annie* and *Beauty and the Beast*.

WHAT FRIENDS SAY

Mr. Tulkinghorn is always coming by with pointless law documents about Jarndyce and Jarndyce and telling Sir Leicester how important the house is and how important the Dedlocks are and how his father served Sir Leicester's father and blah blah blah. He's not my favorite person, but I don't really like anyone.

BIGGEST EMBARRASSMENT

We have a very impressive and imposing fireplace, and Sir Leicester likes to sit in a great chair by the fire, but I find it rather hot (with my handscreen, which is more beautiful than useful) and have been known to get quite faint, like the faintness of death, and need to be taken to my room. But that was just the one time because I recognized in some of Tulkinghorn's papers the handwriting of the long-lost love of my youth, whose daughter I secretly bore out of wedlock. Are you going to print that?

BIGGEST INDULGENCE

A good trunk in which to store illicit love letters is indispensable. My own letters from Captain Hawdon will probably be found, and my shame published, but at least I have a place for them in the interim.

BIGGEST CHALLENGE

I wonder if our mausoleum is big enough. It could probably be bigger.

LOVING YOUR HOME WITH LITTLE DORRIT

"I love a lot of things about my life because I'm a bafflingly chipper character, given what I have gone through. I was born here in the Marshalsea, which is a debtors' prison in Dickensian London. So yeah: not an ideal real estate situation. I don't really know how we ended up here. Something happened with my father and uncle a while back, and my father landed here. An investment gone wrong? I have no idea. I just try to make the most of it and cook disgusting stews for Dad. The river is close by, which is nice, even if it is filled with dead bodies. Sometimes I find some pleasant sticks down there, which I could arrange in a vase if I had one. The downside of living in a debtors' prison is that you are, you know, in prison. But I try to stay positive. I don't know why. It's just my thing."

Evelyn Waugh, Brideshead Revisited

SEBASTIAN'S (RELOCATED) CASTLE OF CATHOLIC FAMILY ISSUES

Names: Sebastian, the champagne-drinking, teddy-bear-toting son of Lady and Lord Marchmain, who are popularly believed to be a saint and an excommunicated magnifico, respectively, and his college buddy Charles

Location: Not far from Oxford; hidden by a green spur and couched among the lime trees like a hind in the bracken

Size: Too big to survive the Second World War, with two or three lovely lakes

Years lived in: It was all planned and planted a century and a half ago so that, at about this date, it might be seen in its maturity; owned

SOMETIMES YOU'RE LUCKY enough to have a friend with a better house than you. And sometimes you're lucky enough to have a friend with a much better house than you.

Such was the case for Charles Ryder, whose youthful friendship with Lord Sebastian Flyte—and time at Sebastian's extraordinary ancestral estate, Brideshead—expanded his decorating horizons and cultivated his artistic aesthetic. The two men met at Oxford, which, in those days, was still a city of aquatint. In her spacious and quiet streets men walked and spoke as they had done in Newman's day. The town was known for her autumnal mists, her gray springtime, and the rare glory of her summer days, as well as bells that rang out high and clear over her gables and cupolas, exhaling the soft airs of centuries of youth. Sometimes people read books, but mostly they just looked great and sat under trees.

"I'm embarrassed to say that my taste was wretched when I first came to Oxford," says Charles. "I should like to think that I decorated my rooms with Morris stuffs and Arundel prints and that the shelves were filled with seventeenth-century folios and French novels of the second empire in Russia leather and watered silk. Those are things that show that you have good taste, by the way. Instead, I proudly hung a reproduction of Van Gogh's *Sunflowers* over the fire. How basic is that? I also had a screen that was painted with a Provençal landscape and a porcelain figure of Polly Peachum, which stood between black tapers on the chimneypiece. The horror. I'm having rapid heart palpitations just thinking about it now. Can we talk about something else?"

Sebastian's taste was more sophisticated because he was a lord, and lords are classy. His room was filled with a strange jumble of objects—a harmonium in a gothic case, an elephant's-foot wastepaper basket, a dome of wax fruit, two disproportionately large Sèvres vases, framed drawings by Daumier, and a chimneypiece covered in cards of invitation from London hostesses. Although he had the same austere college furniture as everyone else, he added a large luncheon table, at which he could be arrestingly beautiful and entertainingly eccentric. Fond of plovers' eggs, lobster Newburg, and Cointreau, Sebastian made Charles's acquaintance by vomiting into the open window of his ground-floor room (but he did send an enormous number of golden daffodils to apologize).

"Only someone quite special drinks a ridiculous mixture of wines and then vomits into your window," Charles says. "Once my carpet was clean, my eyes were opened to a world of beauty far beyond my wildest imagination."

Charles promptly redecorated his rooms to reflect his more sophisticated aesthetic. He sold his cheesy Provençal screen to his not-terribly-interesting scholar friend Collins and got rid of his meager and commonplace books, including the Medici Press edition of *A Shropshire*

Lad and *Eminent Victorians*, replacing them with new and frivolous books, a box of cigars, a Lalique decanter and glasses, and a human skull resting in a bowl of roses and bearing the motto *"Et in Arcadia ego."*

"The School of Medicine is an excellent place to shop for quirky accessories that remind you that even if you have great style, you are still just going to drop dead one day," he says.

Charles undertook this room makeover around the time he was getting drunk in the middle of every afternoon, which is a thing you do in the halcyon days of youth when you have no idea that there is totally another war coming.

But it was his time at Brideshead that proved to be his real decorating education—and prompted his conversion to the Baroque. An excellent place for drinking Château Peyraguey, eating strawberries, and smoking Turkish cigarettes whilst dressed in dove-gray flannel, white crepe de Chine, and a Charvet tie, the former-castle home of Sebastian's family boasted sheep-cropped knolls, clumps of elms, blue-green shadows of foliage, and a tragic sense of irreparable betrayals.

Now a regretful and disillusioned thirty-nine-year-old military captain with a taste for gin and a serious case of nostalgia, Charles describes his present decorating style as "drab" and "soldierly." His current camp is notable for the wireless, which plays incessantly, as well as the nearby municipal lunatic asylum, where he and his comrades sometimes watch the madmen. But at least he can remember Brideshead. That's something.

A CHAT WITH CHARLES
(WHO BEHIND THAT OLD, ENGLISH, PHLEGMATIC EXTERIOR IS AN ARTIST)

SEBASTIAN'S STYLE

Hmm. Who knows. I guess his ancestors chose everything for the house. The family goes back forever—you can look them up in Debrett's. They liked glittering obelisks, arches, broken pediments, terraces with massive stone ramparts, and hothouses teeming with figs and strawberries. The Soanesque library was quite something, as was the Chinese drawing room, adazzle with gilt pagodas and nodding mandarins, painted paper and Chippendale fretwork. They also favored cornices, Doric temples, ivy-grown arches, coved ceilings frescoed with classic deities and heroes, vast fireplaces of sculptured marble, gilt mirrors, scagliola pilasters, and false domes that invoke the cupolas of Chambord. I mean, not really, but nice try.

IMPORTANT INFLUENCES

His narcissism, certainly. But a transfixing and charming narcissism that paired well with Burgundy. And Catholicism. There's an art nouveau chapel attached to Brideshead: a wedding gift from Lord Marchmain to Lady Marchmain. He never came home from the war—the Great one, not this one—and just decided to live with his lover in Italy because that's what absent Catholic patriarchs do. So no one really used the chapel. Sebastian went in there sometimes. I should have known he would end up a total mess in a monastery in Tunisia.

HIS INSPIRATION

Sebastian and his family liked the Painted Parlor, a spacious octagon with a dome decorated with prim Pompeian figures in pastoral groups. We would hang out in there and drink. It was cozy. The satinwood and ormolu furniture, the carpet, the hanging bronze candelabrum, and the mirrors and sconces were all the design of one illustrious hand. It was a place of such enchantment to me, sort of like before the Fall, or like a pastoral idyll, but with really unhappy people in it.

KEY FEATURES

The fountain was an incredible feature—a life-giving spring, you might say, if you were a writer who occasionally got a bit carried away and then

repented his purple prose later in life. A century ago, one of Sebastian's ancestors found it in a piazza in southern Italy and bought it, imported it, and re-erected it here. You should always keep your eyes peeled for great finds like fountains when you travel. One day, when the air was heavy with all the scents of summer, I sketched it, and it turned out to be a very passable echo of Piranesi. If you don't know who that is, you probably didn't go to Oxford.

IMPORTANT PIECES

Sebastian's sister Julia. She was witty as well as ornamental. If you're a man, and you're in love with a man—if you have a friend, you know, who is in that situation—you can just substitute his sister for him, particularly if they look quite a lot alike.

WHAT FRIENDS SAY

They always liked the wine cellar, which was running low but still had enough wine to last ten years. Sebastian and I drank about a dozen bottles each night, but who was counting? Alcoholism is for poor people who don't have epicene beauty and castles.

BIGGEST EMBARRASSMENT

The thinly veiled emotional manipulation and resentment that defined all social interactions at the house. I thought that my dad was bad, with his terrible sense of humor and total lack of appreciation for art. But no. The Marchmains really set the bar.

PROUDEST DIY

I painted a romantic landscape on the panels in a small room opening on the colonnade. It was a summer scene of white clouds and blue distances with an ivy-clad ruin in the foreground, rocks, and a waterfall affording a rugged introduction to the receding parkland behind. I found ideas on Houzz and Design*Sponge, but some were rather jejune.

BIGGEST CHALLENGE

The kind of self-loathing only the very rich can muster; that is a challenge.

PLANS FOR THE FUTURE

There are no plans for the future. There is no future. Everything was better in the past.

DECORATING CHALLENGES
WITH DOROTHEA BROOKE

"I have no dreams of being praised above other women, but I feel that there is always something better which I might have done, if I had only been better and known better. I think we privileged people deserve to be beaten out of our beautiful houses with a scourge of small cords. Or if there aren't any small cords, maybe just other kinds of cords? I can't remember a thing about the décor at Lowick, but I remember my late husband Edward's gloomy old study and all his blasted notebooks and papers for his *Key to All Mythologies*. People think that if you write something in a Moleskine, it's suddenly good. So my advice is to try to improve your poor tenants' pigsty cottages if you can, and for god's sake, steer clear of academic men."

F. Scott Fitzgerald, the Great Gatsby

JAY GATSBY'S DESPERATELY SAD
McMANSION OF UNFULFILLED DREAMS

Name: Jay Gatsby (not his real name), former bootlegger turned fantasist turned dead man floating in a pool

Location: West Egg, New York; less fashionable than East Egg, though this is a mostly superficial tag to express the bizarre and not-a-little-sinister contrast between them

Size: Perfect for huge parties on summer nights

Years lived in: Not long enough to really matter; owned but mortgaged to the hilt

WHEN JAY GATSBY was house hunting, he tried to imagine the area as an old island that flowered once for Dutch sailors' eyes, but he didn't really know much about the Dutch. A recent New York transplant from god-knows-where, he needed the perfect house for a new phase in his life.

What he found was a one-billion-square-foot home with Marie Antoinette music rooms, Restoration salons, gold bathrooms, and a charming coastal location. This not-insignificant real estate investment was motivated by his desire to be close to Daisy, the love interest of his youth and the wife of sadistic Yale graduate and racist Tom Buchanan. It was important for Gatsby to have an excellent vantage point on the Buchanans' cheerful red-and-white Georgian colonial on the other side of the bay.

He also wanted a house where he could entertain—just in case Daisy decided to leave her gilded cage and show up at one of his lavish and emotionally bankrupt events. The mansion's cavernous marble foyer proved an excellent space for welcoming anonymous revelers, and the open-plan kitchen was ideal for a catering staff charged with preparing two dinners per guest. Sometimes his guests got into fights with one another and drove drunk, but that was all just part of the fun of the Roaring Twenties.

Gatsby's friend and neighbor Nick Carraway, who comes from a family of prominent, well-to-do people in a Middle Western city, was kind enough to give us a sense of the doomed protagonist's domestic world.

A CHAT WITH NICK
(OTHERWISE KNOWN AS "OLD SPORT")

GATSBY'S STYLE

I'd say that his style was nouveau riche crossed with a sense of futility in an increasingly alienating and materialistic world. Like a bottle of champagne left open in the sun for several days. He liked having at least one chandelier in every room, and he was fond of marble lions. He was also a big fan of lawns, like Tom and Daisy's, which started at the beach and ran toward the front door for a quarter of a mile, jumping over sundials and brick walls and burning gardens and drifting up the side of the house in bright vines as though from the momentum of its run, but I was always like: Christ, you guys are wasting so much water with your stupid lawn.

HIS INSPIRATION

First and foremost, the Bellagio in Las Vegas. He thought that place was super classy. But he was also inspired by an abiding and fruitless longing for something that never really existed. The house was his way of being near Daisy, my selfish and vain cousin and cipher extraordinaire. She laughs a lot because she's horribly sad. And she got pissed at me for missing her wedding because I wasn't back from the war. I mean, honestly. At any rate, it's hard to say what kind of color palette results from the disappointment of youthful love.

IMPORTANT INFLUENCES

In my younger and more vulnerable years, my father gave me some advice: Decorate your home to reflect your personality. This was hard for Gatsby, as he didn't really know what his personality was, but he read *Town & Country* to get a sense of what a proper society house looks like. He also

flipped through *Kinfolk* once and insisted that his bartenders serve cocktails in mason jars for a little while after that. And he was influenced by the death-bound stare of Dr. T. J. Eckleburg, which you'll remember as one of the ways that you learned about symbols in eighth grade.

FAVORITE ELEMENT

His blue lawn. He liked to stand out there and look at Daisy's dock. He was obsessed with that dock. He went on and on about how he believed in the green light, the orgiastic future that year by year recedes before us, and how it eluded us then, but that's no matter—tomorrow we will run faster, stretch out our arms farther . . . And one fine morning . . . But I was just like, was green the best color choice for the light? I would have gone in another direction. Maybe a nice, bright yellow.

WHAT FRIENDS SAY

What, the people at his gleaming, dazzling parties? Please. They just came to drink his booze and vomit in the shrubs trimmed in the shapes of dollar signs and swans. We all know that Gatsby had no friends, except maybe me, and I'm just an ambivalent mediating figure between the reader and Gatsby's story. I don't even get drunk all that often.

BIGGEST EMBARRASSMENT

The location. You have to travel through a place called the Valley of Ashes to get to the house. I mean, come on. You'd have thought that such a heavy-handed metaphor would have turned him off to the whole enterprise, but no.

PROUDEST DIY

I would say himself. He was kind of a DIY project. He had a Pinterest board that helped him figure out what to wear and how to act and how to throw a party and everything. Otherwise, I really did encourage him to take up a hobby to fill the empty hours of his existence: Maybe spend some time working on the house, beefing up the sparse ivy, or putting in a raised flower bed and planting some leafy greens—but that proved unsuccessful. I thought we might reclaim some lumber from a barn and build a new frame for his waterbed, but he just wanted to stand on his lawn and stare off across the water.

BIGGEST INDULGENCE

His self-absorption. Oh, you mean in terms of décor? He liked French doors. He thought they seemed very French. And the pool, although he might not have liked it so much had he known it would be the site of a melodramatic murder-suicide.

BIGGEST CHALLENGE

He struggled with clutter. Had his life not been cut tragically short, I would have told him to read *The Life-Changing Magic of Tidying Up: The Japanese Art of Decluttering and Organizing*, which you may have heard of if you're alive on this planet. His issue with clutter manifested itself in several ways, but he had a particular issue with clothes. He had all these shirts of sheer linen and thick silk and fine flannel—shirts with stripes and scrolls and plaids in coral and apple-green and lavender and faint orange, and monograms of Indian blue, and, well—you get the idea. They represented the gaping void at the heart of consumer culture, as you'll also remember from eighth grade.

BEST ADVICE

I don't really have any advice. I'm kind of a mess myself.

INTERLUDE: FAIRY-TALE HOMES

Fairy-tale homes are chock-full of decorating inspiration—and constantly under siege by children. No one understands this better than the Mama Bear of "The Three Bears" and the witch in "Hansel and Gretel." Although their houses may not be child friendly, they meet the needs of their owners and reflect their unique style.

WITCH: Kids. Don't even get me started. I put my whole heart and soul into that house. It was my forever home. It had my forever kitchen. I chose my materials carefully: mostly bread, with a roof made of cake and transparent windows of sugar.
MAMA BEAR: Those were the original sugar windows, too, weren't they?
WITCH: Yes. Absolutely. You wouldn't catch me with those awful new windows they make today. Cheap garbage.

MAMA BEAR: Your house had such curb appeal.

WITCH: It really was so much better than the woodcutter and his wife's place—that family had no taste at all. I mean, they may have been starving, but make an effort, if only for your neighbors.

MAMA BEAR: You have such a colorful, maximalist aesthetic. To combine bread and cake. But you pull it off. It's not over-the-top, which is hard to say of many confection-based domiciles.

WITCH: Thanks. That means a lot to me.

MAMA BEAR: But then: those kids.

WITCH: God, then those little brats came along and started eating the siding right off my house. "I'll eat a piece of the roof, and, Gretel, you can try the window," said this Hansel kid. Then he broke off a piece of my roof. I swear to god. Do you know how expensive it is to get a new roof? I'm not in a position to take on a project like that right now. I have a bunch of new curses to learn.

MAMA BEAR: It really is beyond anything.

WITCH: The girl broke a windowpane. I'm sorry, but even in the face of abandonment and exposure, you need to respect private property. I don't want to hear about your villainous stepmother. I'm busy being a witch.

MAMA BEAR: I get it. And it really should be said that you are quite the hostess. They could have just knocked on the door like proper guests.

WITCH: Yes, I ended up inviting them in and feeding them a wonderful meal of milk and pancakes with sugar, apples, and nuts. "You won't meet with any harm here," I said. Tasty little morsels.

MAMA BEAR: Ha! That's a good one.

WITCH: I was just thankful to have the shed on the property. It was a smart investment. Nothing fancy, but big enough to lock up the little boy and attempt to fatten him.

MAMA BEAR: And your oven. For baking.

WITCH: That oven was a splurge. A Dacor with a *secondary oven*. And an iron door you can really slam shut. Excellent for a sizable Thanksgiving turkey—or children. But then, of course, you have had some issues with your place, too.

MAMA BEAR: I did. What is it about human children these days, that they just think they can invade your house when you're away? Is there some sort of sign that says

YEAH, GO AHEAD AND COME ON IN AND MESS UP ALL OUR CHAIRS AND BEDS AND EVERYTHING???

WITCH: I sure as hell don't recall putting up any such sign at my place.

MAMA BEAR: Goldilocks just marched right in. Ate our porridge, too.

WITCH: You don't say.

MAMA BEAR: On my honor. I had set it out nicely—you know how fond I am of a well-set table. It really is a way of maintaining order in a disordered world filled with entitled blond youths.

WITCH: It's so hard to introduce children into a meticulously crafted environment.

MAMA BEAR: Yep. Next thing you know, they're demanding that you paint them a chalkboard wall so they can write crap on it.

WITCH: What do they have to say? They're kids. They should be eaten, not heard.

MAMA BEAR: You can get the leather sofa instead of the fabric, you can make sure you have bins for all their toys, you can get a storage ottoman or two, but they're still just going to take over.

WITCH: I tell you, I have had to look at a lot of baby pictures over the years and ooh and aah and pretend that the little creatures were adorable, but we all have our limits.

II.

CRAZY CASTLES

KING ARTHUR'S BATTLEFIELD-INSPIRED, HYPERMASCULINE MYTHIC CASTLE

Name: Arthur, king of the Britons, warrior, cuckold, and all-around great guy

Location: Not at all clear, although people have rather strong opinions on the subject

Size: Suited to a round table and many knights

Years lived in: Always; owned

KING ARTHUR'S well-known battle exploits often take him far from home, so creating a comfortable domestic space was particularly important to him. He wanted something romantic and magnificent with a French influence.

"Please—call me Arthur," he says. "I'm all about equality. But also about being king."

Arthur has been fortunate to spend time in the much sought-after Avalon neighborhood, which is not to be confused with the luxury apartment buildings in New York City. Sometimes bucolic, sometimes pastoral, and always filled with fruit trees, the island of Avalon is an excellent place to forge magical swords or to recover from battle wounds. But he was looking for something different for his permanent residence, and he found that Camelot satisfied nearly every item on his wish list.

"I really wanted marble countertops in the kitchen," he says. "I had to have them. My whole life depended on whether I had marble countertops. But in the end, I was willing to compromise and settle for rough-hewn raw stone."

Then it was just a matter of decorating in a style that reflects his militant, monarchical masculinity.

"When you leave the battlefield behind, you miss all the blood and mutilated corpses, so I wanted to incorporate some of those elements into my décor, without overdoing it. A few red velvet cushions invoke the bodies of dying men and add a touch of heroic flair."

Arthur also added some flair to the outdoor jousting space in the form of forged steel planters influenced by the work of David Smith and Richard Serra.

"I wanted the yard to say: *I am a man, and I have a blowtorch.*"

A CHAT WITH ARTHUR

HIS STYLE

A magnificent throne is important, of course. Towers, for both aesthetic purposes and for locking people up. But for me, the communal dining space is most important. Camelot has an open plan; the flow from the dining room to the living room is excellent. You can really relax with your mates after slaughtering some people and claiming some land. I like big, dark rooms that smell of roasting meat and post-battle man sweat. We watch the fool, drink a lot, and talk about which women need to be saved.

IMPORTANT INFLUENCES

I'm influenced by war, which, as we all know, is an excellent way for men to bond. I'm also a big fan of nationalist fantasies of English superiority. Otherwise, I'm influenced by Graceland, as it has come to my attention that humans love saint-like figures who supposedly never die.

FAVORITE ELEMENT

If you're a warrior, you really need to mount some weapons on your walls. Otherwise, how will your visitors know what you do? I have a number of lovely swords and shields that I have arranged in a kind of weapon cluster. You want to polish them periodically—and be sure to wash off the blood and guts of your enemies before hanging them.

UNIQUE ELEMENTS

Gosh—everything. Everyone knows that Camelot is the greatest castle ever. I mean, you may have a castle, and it's probably a fine castle, but it's no Camelot.

WHAT FRIENDS SAY

Lancelot likes the dusty, decorative suits of armor and sometimes asks if he can borrow one to go fight in a battle. He comes over a lot to talk to Guinevere. They favor one of the castle's isolated and private sunrooms, and it is indeed a magnificent room—so light and airy. They get along so well. He's such a great friend.

PROUDEST DIY

The kitchen makes a very juicy turkey leg. Does that count?

BIGGEST INDULGENCE

I designated one of the large stone rooms as a "man space"—apart from the rest of the world, which you might also say is a man space. Sometimes you need a place where you don't have to hear about your "Honey Do" list, am I right?

PLANS FOR THE FUTURE

Maybe get some more fields? We have some lovely green fields around the castle. Sometimes I go out and stand in the fields, just to remind myself of how many there are. But I could probably have more.

DECORATING WITH THE CREW FROM *THE DECAMERON*

"Our villa is secluded and quiet—the perfect place to tell stories. It's a lot like *Under the Tuscan Sun*, but instead of Cortona, we're outside Florence, and instead of the sun, there is the plague."

Bram Stoker, Dracula

COUNT DRACULA'S COFFIN-FILLED
CASTLE OF CASEMENTS AND CASUALTIES

Name: Count Dracula, vampire to end all vampires (I see you, YA novels)

Location: In the snowy mountaintops of Transylvania

Size: Big

Years lived in: That's a hard question to answer without inspiring disbelief; owned

ALTHOUGH YOUNG LAWYER Jonathan Harker had read about Transylvania in the British Library, nothing could prepare him for the real thing—or for the extraordinary architectural marvel he would encounter as the guest-slash-prisoner of Count Dracula.

The green sloping land around Dracula's castle is full of forests and woods, with here and there steep hills crowned with clumps of trees or with farmhouses. These hills rise up to the lofty steeps of the Carpathian mountains, which tower above with all their glorious colors, deep blue and purple in the shadows of the peaks, green and brown where grass and rock mingle. A cock crows with preternatural shrillness through the clear morning air, and there are many jagged rocks and pointed crags.

"I love a jagged rock and a pointed crag," Jonathan discourses.

Nestled among the wild and hypnotic howls of wolves and the agonized cries of women, the ancient castle boasts broken walls, a gloomy courtyard, great round arches, worn-down stone carvings, imposing fireplaces, bars on the windows, and many chains and bolts. The library contains a large number of English books and periodicals, and Dracula enjoys lying on the sofa and reading riveting things like railway timetables and reports of royal commissions.

Jonathan is particularly struck by the brilliant moonlight that bathes the beautiful expanse.

"Anywhere can have excellent light," he says. "But few places have moonlight capable of casting phantom shadows that fill you with a sense of doom."

In spite of the castle's extraordinary evidences of wealth, some "odd deficiencies" add to its nightmarish character. The enormous front door has no bell or knocker as you enter freely and of your own will, and there are no servants. On chilly nights—and really on most nights—the wind breathes cold through the broken battlements and casements.

"It's a simple insulation issue, but I haven't looked into it yet as I find I'm dealing with bigger issues," Jonathan says. "Like the fact that the count crawls down the castle walls."

The castle's curb appeal is bolstered by a narrow ledge of stone that runs around the south side of the building. The stones are big and roughly cut, and the mortar has by process of time been washed away between them. Jonathan enjoys venturing out onto this ledge and, trying his best not to look at the awful depths below, gradually making his way to the window of Dracula's room, which sports quirky details like a great heap of gold in one corner, odd things that seem never to have been used, and dust. Jonathan's own room is well lighted and warmed with a log fire, and the centuries-old curtains, the upholstery of the chairs and sofa, and the hangings of his bed are of the costliest and most beautiful fabrics.

"I saw something like them in Hampton Court, but they were worn and frayed and moth-eaten," he says. "So I said as much in my review on Yelp."

A CHAT WITH JONATHAN

DRACULA'S STYLE

He loves that his house is old and big. He himself is of an old family, and to live in a new house would kill him. "A house cannot be made habitable in a day, and after all, how many days go by to make up a century," Dracula likes to say. He enjoys frowning walls and dark window openings. Of course, you want a castle that inspires fear, horror, and wonder—something a little vampy. But you don't want to tip over into the domain of theme restaurants. This isn't the World Famous Jekyll and Hyde Club, people. Cheap animated mummies are not okay.

IMPORTANT INFLUENCES

We agree that the Bran, Poenari, and Corvin Castles are all quite nice. Bran thinks quite a lot of itself. But Dracula's castle really takes its cue from the surrounding area. It's quite impregnable on three sides as it's located on the edge of a terrible precipice, and a stone falling from a window would fall a thousand feet without touching anything! Below, there are silver threads where the rivers wind in deep gorges through the forests. *It is gorges.* Get it? Christ, I should put that on a T-shirt.

FAVORITE ELEMENT

There is a portion of the castle that was evidently occupied in bygone days, judging from the relatively comfortable furniture that is now ravaged by time and moths. Sometimes I write there, at a little oak table, overcome by a loneliness that chills my heart and makes my nerves tremble. There is also a lovely dining room where the Count never dines. And the castle has a number of mirrors that seem to be defective. Maybe we should return them.

POTENTIAL IMPROVEMENTS

Dracula loves heavy doors, so we could put in more heavy doors. And maybe we could add more nails. You can't go wrong with studding things with large iron nails.

WHAT FRIENDS SAY

Mina would find the place intriguing, but she's kind of preoccupied with a friend in England right now, so her thoughts tend more to garlic and wolves than interior design. But I think she'd say that wolf figurines can make nice accent pieces. There are some whimsical and not-horrifying options in Target's Threshold line.

BIGGEST EMBARRASSMENT

Let me not think of it. My heart grows cold at the thought. It's enough to inspire a violent fit of hysterics and uncontrollable emotional eruptions.

BIGGEST INDULGENCE

I would say the ancient, ruined, tomb-like chapel at the bottom of a dark, tunnel-like passage through which comes a deathly, sickly odor of old earth newly turned. The space is decorated with fragments of old coffins. Transylvanian nobles don't like to think that their bones may be among the common dead. No, siree. The count has his own box, with a lid pierced with holes. It is bespoke.

BIGGEST CHALLENGE

Sexy lady vampires, definitely. They are terrifying.

BEST ADVICE

Steer clear of trends that refuse to die. Take terrariums, for example. You might think: Oh, they're sort of creepy, these little self-contained worlds of rocks and plants. Kind of Transylvanian. They might add an element of terror, dreadful pleasure, and languorous ecstasy. But no: Dracula absolutely does not allow terrariums in the castle. You get a terrarium, and it's a slippery slope to macramé. And that's some diabolical wickedness.

LOVING YOUR HOME WITH MANFRED, PRINCE OF OTRANTO

"A castle should be defined by its medieval gloomth. If your imagination runs to an armor-clad giant's foot or a portrait of your grandfather that utters a deep sigh and heaves its breast, great. If you fancy a royal bedchamber in which no one ever sleeps, I say go ahead. But look out for enormous helmets. If they're not properly secured, they can fall, and you'll end up with a mangled and disfigured corpse."

William Shakespeare, Macbeth

LADY MACBETH'S MURDEROUS MANSION OF BLOOD AND DEATH

Names: Lady Macbeth, witchlike queen of undaunted mettle known for her strong opinions on masculinity and fondness for multiple homicide, and her husband, Macbeth (tragic figure)

Location: Scotland, near a heath and not far from a forest

Size: Kingly

Years lived in: Since the Macbeths' recent regicide; owned (at least for now)

IT HAS BEEN A NONSTOP YEAR for Lady Macbeth, whose husband's recent promotion to Thane of Cawdor and then to King of Scotland meant a new home for them both. After grueling negotiations with their movers and the weird sisters out on the heath, they said good-bye to their only-okay castle in Inverness and moved into the royal domicile, recently vacated by Duncan, whom they killed while he was visiting them.

"I know what you're going to say: It's a total violation of the codes of hospitality to murder your guest," she says. "But it's a rat race out there, and I wasn't about to just wait around for my husband to become king. We wanted to be proactive and really blue sky it. In the end, bloody murder seemed like the best option."

Lady Macbeth "leans in" not only in the professional world but also in her approach to decorating the new castle.

"There are challenges with inheriting a property that belonged to someone you plotted to stab repeatedly while he slept," she says. "You want to put your own stamp on it and make it personal, but you also want to respect the memory of the former king to keep the rabble happy."

Macbeth is also a big fan of the property, which boasts a large dining room, dark and foreboding chambers, drippy candles, and lots of thunder and lightning. Lady Macbeth hopes to use the dining room for more hostessing in the future. When it comes to tablescapes, she favors a rustic vibe and is always on the lookout for pinecones, bark, pilots' fingers, and other things one can generally find in cauldrons.

"The good news is that we don't have to have Malcolm over anymore because he's raising an army against us," she says. "God, he's *so* boring. Good luck with your boring army, Malcolm."

A CHAT WITH LADY MACBETH

HER STYLE

I like bearskin rugs from very large bears, red velvet drapes, knives with bone handles, and statues that are extra menacing. When it comes to floral arrangements, my taste tends toward snapdragons, burrs, and those flowers that are green and spiky and don't look like flowers at all.

IMPORTANT INFLUENCES

I'm inspired by the aesthetic of shrieking owls and crying crickets, but that can be challenging to translate into a scheme for an antechamber. I love an industrial vibe—lots of metal, high ceilings, exposed pipes, brick walls, a concrete floor, and maybe a Sputnik chandelier. What we have here is more classic, but that was Duncan! I once saw an abattoir that I thought was just lovely.

INTERESTING FEATURES

Our old castle featured a drunken porter who mostly just talked about erectile dysfunction, but I kind of miss his high jinks. Here, we have some nice Disney-esque turrets where I hope to hide some bodies one day.

IMPORTANT PIECES

Last week, I went to an estate sale for yet another guy killed in battle and picked up some fluffy Mongolian lamb pillow covers. We also have a collection of gorgeous severed heads. Severed heads aren't just for sticking on pikes anymore—you can bring them into the home as memorable embellishments. For example, if you're thinking about styling a bookshelf, I suggest a neat stack of coffee-table books with an eye of newt and toe of frog on top.

WHAT FRIENDS SAY

That they're sorry, but something came up and they can't come over after all.

KEY FEATURES

I love our plush sofa by the hearth, but Macbeth's taste is a bit, well, *soldierly*, and he wanted to reupholster it in camo. I told him absolutely not.

We also have some gorgeous family crests, although they're not exactly ours because of the whole usurpation thing.

BIGGEST SPLURGE

After the spirits unsexed me and filled me from the crown to the toe top-full with direst cruelty, I decided that I needed a dedicated room for myself. I have a proper bar in there and a lot of taxidermy, including a wildebeest and a squirrel paddling a canoe.

PROUDEST DIY

I adore my decorative raven, which I actually shot and stuffed myself. Macbeth doesn't really like taxidermy, but he always says, "Happy wife, happy life!"

BIGGEST EMBARRASSMENT

Banquo's ghost, no question. The absolute worst thing about killing people is that they *always* turn into ghosts and show up at your dinner parties. Macbeth really lost it, which was mortifying for me, particularly as I wasn't feeling superconfident about my soufflé that evening.

BIGGEST CHALLENGE

Finding a comfortable bed for the master suite. We don't sleep well. Apparently, I have been walking around at night, folding pieces of paper and trying to wash imaginary blood off my hands. I just finished Arianna Huffington's latest book, which has some great tips about how to get the best sleep for maximum rich-white-person success, but my husband is all, "SLEEP NO MORE! MACBETH DOES MURDER SLEEP." He thinks that the problem is reckoning with our heinous crimes, but I think we're dealing with a mattress issue. It's time to go Tempur-Pedic.

PLANS FOR THE FUTURE

I'd like a red Sencor toaster. And maybe central heating; it's cold as balls here. I don't know if this is our dream home, but it's great for now—and much better than Macduff's castle, although we haven't been over there recently.

BEST ADVICE

Just because we're in Scotland doesn't mean that you have to incorporate a lot of tartan. You don't need your home to look like a university club filled with asshole bankers. Hey, when it comes to decorating, fair is foul, and foul is fair, if you know what I mean, and I think you do.

DECORATING CHALLENGES WITH HAMLET

"The hardest thing at Elsinore is maintaining an orderly graveyard. We have this showstopping graveyard, but it is rather crowded, and I have the feeling it may become even more crowded here soon. Yorick was buried there, the king's jester. Alas, poor Yorick. I found his skull the other day. I suppose I could have held onto it—maybe set up a nice tableau with some books and oysters in the manner of a Dutch still life. I should have thought of that. Well, I have a fencing match to get to."

Charlotte Brontë, Jane Eyre

JANE AND EDWARD'S FIRE-RAVAGED GOTHIC RUIN

Names: Jane, former long-suffering governess, and Edward, ill-tempered man

Location: Yorkshire, England

Size: Three stories high, of proportions not vast, though considerable: a gentleman's manor house, not a nobleman's seat

Years lived in: Probably since William the Conqueror; owned

JANE AND EDWARD'S charming ruin, Thornfield Hall, may no longer be their primary residence, but it persists as a reminder of the extraordinary beauty of the great houses of the English countryside. Jane recalls days spent tutoring Edward's neglected and isolated ward, Adèle, in one of the castle's many sitting rooms. Edward remembers evenings next to the fire, wallowing in misery. Their housekeeper, Mrs. Fairfax, remembers a lot of dusting.

When Thornfield burned to the ground, its style was already rather outdated. Edward had made few changes to the house, and in time it took on an old-fashioned vibe some might describe as "creepy" but which Jane characterizes as "retro." Before their interrupted wedding, Edward had planned to refresh the dining room with a regal shade of red, but Jane asked him to reconsider the color palette as she'd spent much of her childhood locked in a red room by an evil aunt. Edward's taste tends to run to jewel-encrusted goblets, mahogany armchairs, and tapestries of King Harold being gouged in the eye.

Even with a castle, Edward says that he had still faced some "small space" decorating challenges —particularly in setting up the room in which he secretly confined his hysterical and excessively sexual wife Bertha, far off in some unvisited part of the house. Loyal servant Grace Poole took it upon herself to design this studio apartment. In consultation with Edward, she decided to line the walls with dirty mattresses and to cover the floor in rags. Thick damask curtains in a calming shade of green muffled the sounds of Bertha's sobs and cut her off from the outside world.

A CHAT WITH JANE

THEIR STYLE

Edward and I think of our style as sort of "medieval suit of armor meets oppressive and claustrophobic wealth." Edward traveled a lot when he was younger, and although he doesn't like to talk about it much, he brought back some souvenirs—quirky vases and that sort of thing—that I try to display with some of our more traditional items, like mounts, large brass candlesticks, and paintings of dead relatives. I like a lot of light, probably because it helps me to think of God and try to forgive him for taking my friend Helen Burns from me when we were young. She died of consumption, which was strange as there was an outbreak of typhus at the time. But she was unique, much like my evolving decorating style. Our new place has much better light than Thornfield, and it has a roof.

INSPIRATION

Edward wanted to model Thornfield on a place called Otranto, but he was also inspired by moldering crypts. He loves animal skeletons, old leather-bound books, and his dog, but I try to find inspiration everywhere. I love color and pattern because I've always worn drab gray dresses. And I find big fireplaces inspiring as I was cold as a child. Child abuse really makes you reevaluate how you think about space and décor. Lowood School had a minimalist style: hard beds for all us girls, no hot water, little food, unwarranted corporal punishment, and rampant deadly illnesses. But I guess those last things don't have to do with design!

FAVORITE ELEMENT

I used to really like to read in the library. We were planning to breathe life into the space with a few new design elements, but we never got the chance since we had to cancel our wedding and I had to flee into the night. There never seems to be enough time for home improvements! I wanted the library to be the perfect retreat: a place where Edward could brood about the past and reflect on how the world has wronged him.

WHAT FRIENDS SAY

We didn't really have a lot of friends over, per se. As I may have mentioned, my friend Helen was the only person who ever loved me, and no one else could ever be quite so fabulous. And Edward has never been much of a host. He has been described as "Byronic," which is to say that he's border-line sociopathic and inclined to anger and violence, but in a way that naïve young women hundreds of years from now will probably still find sexy. Hey, I get it, ladies—I was there.

BIGGEST EMBARRASSMENT

Well, it was embarrassing when Thornfield burned down. That Bertha—or Antoinetta, or whatever—she proved to be a real problem. Total mad-woman in the attic, if you know what I mean.

PROUDEST DIY

Edward and I are not big DIY people. He's generally too busy drinking and riding around the countryside, and I have my sketching. We did try to fix a tree on the property that had been struck by lightning, but it was no use. The lightning really did a number on it. It might have been a symbol of what was to come, but I'm probably reading too much into it.

BIGGEST INDULGENCE

A few antiques we bought with my unexpected inheritance. The money came completely out of the blue! One moment I was working as a schoolmistress in the middle of nowhere, resisting the pressure to marry a good Christian man with no personality whatsoever, and the next thing I knew, I was an heiress! And, of course, then I returned to Edward, and he has boatloads of cash, so we've been able to spend my money on gorgeous things to accessorize our new house. We lost most of his stuff in the fire, but far from a melodramatic tragedy that effectively disposed of an unvalued life, it was a great opportunity to reimagine what we want our home to really say about us. We're using the money to expand our collection of antique Roman coins and pottery shards, as well as to acquire some Egyptian rarities. Edward has a friend who's a tomb raider, and he brings us back the loveliest things.

BEST ADVICE

Seek out advice about what works (and what doesn't) in a really large house. I've learned a lot in transitioning from Thornfield to our new place. It's always a challenge to make forty-five rooms feel homey and warm, and I worry sometimes that I haven't gotten it quite right. And Edward wasn't much help to me initially because he was blind. Didn't have much of an eye, you might say! No opinions at all about whether we should go with fabric headboards or more traditional four-poster beds in the guest rooms. But really, my advice is: Don't be afraid to shape your house into the kind of home you've always wanted. And if you hear maniacal laughter in the middle of the night, don't ignore it.

Mary Shelley, Frankenstein

VICTOR'S CHARNEL HOUSE–ESQUE
HIDEOUS PROGENY OF A PALACE

Name: Victor Frankenstein, widower (Elizabeth was great), member of a distinguished family, and mocker of the stupendous mechanism of the Creator of the world (Genevese by birth)

Location: Ingolstadt, in the Odenwald mountains, Germany

Size: Resembling the imaginative capacity of man

Years lived in: Since a resistless and almost frantic impulse urged him to undertake his home makeover; owned

WE ALL WANT TO ACCOMPLISH some great purpose. For seeker-of-knowledge Victor Frankenstein, his home was an excellent place to start. His castle welcomes you with misery and despair, its cold, gray stones suggesting an owner of sometimes violent temper, with passions vehement.

"I am inspired by wonder," he says. "Homes that are truly marvelous and take an irresistible hold on my imagination. I also like gargoyles. Those crazy little guys."

The castle was enlarged and modernized in the fifteenth century, but Victor saw the potential for further improvements. He worked for two years to bestow animation on the lifeless matter of his domestic space. As rain pressed dismally against the austere steel windowpanes, he listened to "Puttin' on the Ritz" and went through fabric swatches and blood-repellent laminate floor options with indefatigable zeal, finally realizing the gratifying consummation of his toils as the moon gazed on his midnight labors.

You might say that his laboratory for the study of alchemy and natural philosophy is "where the magic happens." Here, in a solitary chamber, or rather cell, at the top of the house and separated from all the other apartments by a gallery and staircase, he undertook his work of inconceivable difficulty and labor, which he prefers not to discuss in detail. He will say that he has found a number of treasures in dissecting rooms and slaughterhouses, as well as in vaults and charnel houses, which he describes as "vivid" in style. He found a number of accessories in the Alexander McQueen for Kohl's line and invested in some art by Damien Hirst.

"The skulls, not the butterflies," he says.

Whenever he struggled with a space, he thought of the bleak sides of woodless mountains, dreary nights, and beakers.

"Who was I? What was I? Whence did I come? What was my destination? These questions are central to both experimental science and personal style," he says. "I am enchanted by the corpses of executed criminals. The structure of the human frame. All those different parts that make up a whole, like FLOR carpet tiles."

And he turned to the Container Store's storage solutions to create an almost clinically organized space.

"Where are my hearts? My eyeballs? My severed hands?" he asks. "I need to be able to find a foot if I need one. Everything has its place."

He will admit that he had a countenance expressive of a calm, settled grief when he realized that he had to pick up and install the storage system himself—he was outside the delivery zone—but this proved to be a project suited to his meticulous personality.

For Victor, design is a way of creating something beautiful. Or not. Depending.

"If you don't have a design plan, you can end up with a startling catastrophe on your hands," he says. "You want to come out the victor. Oh god, is my name a *pun*? That is seriously just occurring to me now."

A CHAT WITH VICTOR

HIS STYLE

Textile-wise, I like patterns that gratuitously harass the heart. When I find the right one, a strange multiplicity of sensations seizes me. I love electricity—not light fixtures, you know, but theories of electricity that allow for deformed and abortive creations. I like a majestic aesthetic that recalls the dangerous mysteries of the ocean and snow-capped peaks that are both beautiful and terrifying. Anything that brings to mind the divine glories of heaven and earth. No one can feel more deeply than I the beauties of nature. Except maybe nature. Which I will tame and control like you tame a woman or an unreliable contractor.

HIS INSPIRATION

Certainly ghost stories. I wanted one room that would be perfect for crowding around a blazing wood fire in the evenings and amusing myself with friends, if I decide to make any. I was also inspired by the wildness of Lake Geneva, which is a lovely place to summer, if you know someone with a property there. And if you don't know someone with a property there, you should do something about that immediately.

IMPORTANT INFLUENCES

I'm influenced by Dante's sense that everything is the worst. His design scheme for hell is impressive, to say the least! Also Agrippa, Magnus, and Paracelsus. I like a thoughtfully layered home that suggests agony, torment, and isolation. And I knew that I wanted an all-black kitchen—something very Gothic. I put in antique petit granite, which is like normal granite but petit. When using darker shades, you must honor the architecture of the space. Perhaps you want to put in a black concrete apron sink and a matte black faucet. Great. But just be sure to streamline your surfaces and strike a balance: Maybe paint the cabinets a dark black and the walls a darker shade of black. Then you're ready for accessories—ebony ceramics, black-rimmed baskets, forged steel cutlery, and some good, heavy knives for chopping up the bodies you dig up in the middle of the night.

BIGGEST INDULGENCE

I wanted to re-upholster some old chairs, and when it came to selecting fabrics, I felt as if my soul was grappling with a palpable enemy. But I found consolation for my toils in the form of some nice swatches from Room & Board. I redid the dining room chairs in "Ancient Mariner," a delicious deep blue with distinct hints of doom, and "Prometheus," which is a fierier color. I know that some people would have gone with a simple tan neutral, but I don't want to think of and dilate upon so very hideous an idea.

UNIQUE FEATURE

My bed is incredible. The bed linens are from Godwin Fabrics, and the bed itself is a custom piece by Jacobin Design. I swear, it's so comfortable that I have the wildest dreams. I had one the other night where I thought that I saw Elizabeth in the bloom of health, and I embraced her and kissed her on the lips, and she changed into the corpse of my dead mother. So, like I said: a *really* comfortable bed. With curtains.

BIGGEST CHALLENGE

Sometimes you feel that blank incapability of invention which is the greatest misery of decorating, when dull Nothing replies to your anxious invocations. This happened to me when I was thinking about where to put my operating table in my laboratory. Is it best in the middle of the room to create a sense of flow? Or up against a wall to save space? That was tricky. But these are just the enervating effects of the creative process!

WHAT FRIENDS SAY

I shun my fellow creatures as if I have been guilty of a crime, so I don't know.

PLANS FOR THE FUTURE

Maybe take a break? Just walk around on some ice?

BEST ADVICE

The labor of men of decorating genius, however erroneously directed, scarcely can ever fail in ultimately turning to the solid advantage of mankind. I think. I hope.

DECORATING WITH THE GOVERNESS AT BLY

"The estate seemed fine when I arrived. Big, ugly, and antique, but convenient. I suppose I had dreaded something melancholy, so what greeted me was a good surprise: open windows, fresh curtains, and bright flowers. The crenellated towers were architectural absurdities, to be sure—dating, in their gingerbread antiquity, from a romantic revival that was already a respectable past. But then—stay with me here— I saw this man passing from one of the crenellations to the next, never taking his eyes from me. It was creepy. Like, Udolpho creepy. And I'm in charge of children, so I'm pretty trustworthy, right? Things are changing here. Something is off. I'll keep you posted."

INTERLUDE:
AN IDEAL GOVERNESS'S ROOM

Governesses are not real people, but domestic labor that looks like human women, so you don't need to worry too much about making them comfortable. After all, your precious children will soon be old enough to be sent off to school, and then you can tell your governess to pack up and leave, preferably on a rainy day. Becky Sharp and Jane Eyre offer indispensable advice for decorating a drafty, borderline uninhabitable room that says, "You Were Not Born for This Life, or Maybe You Were, but at Any Rate, Get Used to It."

BECKY: This better not take long as I need to work on my schemes.

JANE: It won't take too long.

BECKY: Good. I have a busy schedule of social climbing.

JANE: So: our rooms. I'll say that my room at Thornfield Hall could have been worse. It wasn't quite as bad as the servants' rooms. They just get a scratchy blanket and a pillow that has been drooled on by countless other strangers.

BECKY: But we are governesses.

JANE: Yes. Not servants. But not quite family either.

BECKY: Exactly. We are one of the most familiar figures in mid-Victorian life and literature. And ideally suited to picaresque narratives, given our lack of resources and family.

JANE: That is true.

BECKY: We can't all be Amelia Sedleys, now, can we? I should be so lucky. But no. I end up at Queen's Crawley, teaching two of Sir Pitt's daughters.

JANE: Sir Pitt is no Rochester.

BECKY: So much mutton in that house.

JANE: As a governess, you're really moving back and forth between your bedroom and your schoolroom. The defining feature of my bedroom is that it was not lit on fire. I can't say the same thing of Edward's.

BECKY: Who lit it on fire?

JANE: I'd rather not talk about it. But fire does not do any favors for décor.

BECKY: I would think not.

JANE: A governess's bedroom is quite important, as she spends a lot of time there. It is her sanctuary, where she can reflect on the poverty that awaits her in middle age.

BECKY: Queen's Crawley is sometimes described as rotten. And indeed, by the lapse of time, and those mutations which age produces in empires, cities, and boroughs, it was no longer so populous a place as it had been in Queen Bess's time.

JANE: It looks like a dump.

BECKY: It was a little bit of a dump. Old baronets and their moldering properties. But Jos didn't work out, so it was as good a place as any to plot next steps.

JANE: And in the meantime, we really only require a schoolroom and a simple bedroom.

BECKY: Yes. When I was at Sir Pitt's place in London—a tall gloomy house between two other tall gloomy houses—I slept in the great front bedroom, where Lady Crawley had slept her last. The bed and chamber were so funereal and gloomy, you might have fancied not only that Lady Crawley died in the room but that her ghost inhabited it. But I thought it was great.

JANE: That's the vibe at Thornfield Hall.

BECKY: There were huge wardrobes, closets, cupboards, locked drawers, dreary pictures, and toilette appointments. The mantelpiece cast up a great black shadow over half of a moldy old sampler, which her defunct ladyship had worked, no doubt, and over two little family pictures of young lads, one in a college gown, and the other in a red jacket like a soldier.

JANE: Always so many samplers. At least get some *new* samplers. We don't need moldy old samplers.

BECKY: Yes.

JANE: When I arrived at Thornfield, Mrs. Fairfax took me to my bedroom. It was the room next to hers—better, she said, than the large front chambers, which had finer furniture but were so dreary and solitary. There was a long gallery into which the bedroom doors opened, and it all looked more like a church than a house. A very chill and vault-like air pervaded the stairs and gallery, suggesting cheerless ideas of space and solitude.

BECKY: These wretched aristocrats can't even heat their houses.

JANE: But the room was okay: small and furnished in an ordinary modern style. Livelier than the wide hall and spacious staircase. It had blue chintz window curtains, papered walls, and a carpeted floor. Much better than Lowood School.

BECKY: That's a *low* bar.

JANE: Ha! Good joke. Their aesthetic was deprivation crossed with typhus.

BECKY: It could always be worse.

JANE: At least a governess has her schoolroom, which we have some control over. We have our chalkboard, our books, and our maps, which show which parts of the world are savage and which are British.

BECKY: For geography. And maybe some dolls and puppets.

JANE: For a puppet show.

BECKY: Yes. As we know all too well, the general idea is that women should be accomplished, not educated. If they are educated, they start saying things. But teach them French. The piano. Dancing and deportment. These things do not disturb the universe.

JANE: Needlework.

BECKY: Exactly. Maybe you end up with a nice cushion cover. What a thrill. Almost enough to distract you from the horrors of our social position.

JANE: Almost. Overall, I favor a plain style in cushion covers. Plain like myself.

BECKY: Yes, a plain governess is always best as she is unlikely to tempt the men of the house.

JANE: That's the thought.

BECKY: You messed that all up.

JANE: I sure did.

III.

URBAN
LIVING

Charles Dickens, Great Expectations

MISS HAVISHAM'S DECAYING DOMICILE OF DISAPPOINTED LOVE

Name: Miss Havisham, corpse-like jilted heiress to a brewery fortune

Size: Not clear as she tends to keep to a few rooms (but big)

Years lived in: Time no longer matters as all the clocks were stopped at twenty minutes to nine; owned

SELF-DESCRIBED "HOMEBODY" Miss Havisham always knew that she would inherit her family's beer business, as well as the manor house adjacent to the brewery buildings. These abandoned structures—which are accented by old, empty casks—provide the perfect counterpoint to the main house's sense of hopelessness and misery. The name "Satis House," which is some foreign language for "enough," was inspired by the idea that whoever owns this house could want nothing else. And Miss Havisham is satisfied indeed: She has cultivated a grave-like domestic aesthetic that suggests the freedom from desire that comes only with death.

This old, dismal brick house has a great many iron bars on it, and some of the windows have been walled up. There is a courtyard in front, which is also barred.

"I like bars on dirty windows," she says. "And rust on bars."

The courtyard is paved, clean, and accented with overgrown grass in every crevice. The property also boasts a rank garden of tangled weeds, an old wall, a detached dwelling house, and a pigeon house blown crooked on its pole and long ago abandoned by any pigeons.

Of course, the challenge to inheriting any manor is making it your own, and she has put her own stamp on Satis House by neglecting it entirely. Daylight is completely excluded from the home's gloomy rooms, and low ceilings suggest the oppressive airlessness of being buried alive.

"I have a total horror of open windows," she says, the fingers on her right hand twitching. "I mean, what a waste of stale air, to just go around throwing your windows open willy-nilly. Sometimes I let Estella open a window so she can yell something out of it, but then terrible gusts of fresh air disrupt all my cobwebs, and I have to put them in the right places again."

When she is not arranging cobwebs, Miss Havisham enjoys emotionally manipulating children and thinking about the man who left her at the altar and ruined her life. Described by others as a waxwork skeleton, a collapsed form, and a witch, Miss Havisham values the peace that her retreat affords.

"Satis House is a place just for myself," she says, flicking a gnat off the rotting wedding dress she wears constantly. "I have the sick fancy to put in a spa bathroom—a real treat, with a sculptural freestanding tub and a steam shower. Hashtag self-care, I always say."

A CHAT WITH MISS HAVISHAM

HER STYLE

I like large rooms lighted with wax candles, long and mysterious passageways, and dust. No Swiffering for me. I say, let it pile up. Sometimes I light a fire in the grate, just to fill the home with smoke like a marsh mist. I prefer to surround myself with pale, destroyed objects that hint at heartbreak and despair. Most afternoons, I just sit at my dressing table and stare at my cadaverous face in my gilded looking glass, but if I'm feeling sprightly, I may walk across the room and pick up my prayer book. Fabric-wise, I'm partial to satin, lace, and silk—all in white. I prefer to have white everything. The color decays and ages in a way that other colors do not, so it's a constant reminder that everything in life is fleeting and just a huge effing disappointment.

IMPORTANT INFLUENCES

Definitely the sartorial. You want to have a complete aesthetic: Your clothing and your home should speak to each other. But life can get very busy—you need to set aside at least eight hours a day to reflect on your lost love—so I favor uniform dressing to streamline my routine. My outfit of choice is my withering bridal gown. Some people just fill their homes with their wedding pictures—yeah, we get it; you're married—but I like a less conventional approach. I accessorize my rotting and paperlike dress with flowers in my hair, a handkerchief, gloves, some bright jewels, and one shoe. I also wear a veil as I'm getting up there, and no one wants to look at the face of a woman in her fifties.

FAVORITE ELEMENT

A good table, where you can force your guests to play cards. Estella likes to play cards. At least, I think she does. I never asked. I also like roaring fires. Sometimes I don't tend mine quite as I should, but I'm sure that won't be a problem.

POTENTIAL IMPROVEMENTS

Things could be more withered and crumbling. I love ruins: ruined buildings, ruined people, ruined lives, ruined dreams. I try to weave that concept into my décor, sometimes with something as simple as an embroidered Etsy throw pillow that reads, LOVE IS LIFE'S JOY or I FUCKING HATE PEOPLE. And I wouldn't mind a pet monkey.

WHAT FRIENDS SAY

That I look nice, and then I say: I look like a yellowing corpse, you liar.

BIGGEST EMBARRASSMENT

That I was jilted by a no-good fortune hunter. And I have some problems with mice and black beetles.

PROUDEST DIY

I am quite skilled at tablescapes. I love a good centerpiece heavily overhung with cobwebs and infested with speckled-legged spiders with blotchy bodies. My real pièce de résistance was for my wedding. You think I was going to let all that go to waste? Christ, no. You don't throw out a perfectly good wedding cake just because you don't actually get married. The moldering bride cake really ties the room together, and one day, when I die, my corpse will be laid out on the table, too—in what you might call the ultimate tablescape.

BIGGEST INDULGENCE

Probably my heartbreak and total retreat from the world, but that is the fault of my illustrious author. I can't believe he was allowed to write female characters like me. At one point, he refers to me as a "grave lady." I mean, come on. He really put the "dick" in "Dickens."

BIGGEST CHALLENGE

The garden. I'd like to do more gardening. For now, the outdoor area is just a miserable corner, a rank ruin of cabbage stalks, and a boxtree that has been badly trimmed—no Edward Scissorhands job there. But I could perhaps put in a pergola, string some Edison bulbs, and do some light entertaining whereby I invite people over and then treat them like dogs in disgrace.

BEST ADVICE

Beware of charming men but not charming wall sconces.

FUTURE PLANS

If I have any free time, maybe I'll reclaim the term "spinster."

LOVING YOUR HOME WITH
TESS OF THE D'URBERVILLES

"My accommodations as a milkmaid were certainly adequate, but that wasn't going to last because of, well, fate. And horrible men. More the latter than the former, if you want my opinion. I really like Stonehenge. Does that count as a house? I mean, we don't really know what it is, right? And it doesn't have a roof, which could be an issue. It might be a tricky place to live, but it's a great place to die."

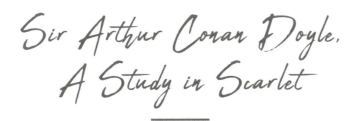

Sir Arthur Conan Doyle, A Study in Scarlet

JOHN AND SHERLOCK'S
BAKER STREET ROOMS FOR RUMINATING

Names: Sherlock Holmes, detective who gets down in the dumps at times and then doesn't open his mouth for days on end, and John Watson, who doesn't know what hit him, roommate-wise

Location: 221B Baker Street, London (or the great cesspool into which all the loungers and idlers of the Empire are irresistibly drained)

Size: Moderate

Years lived in: Not very long; rented from Mrs. Hudson

UPON HIS RETURN from the prolonged hardships of Afghanistan, wounded army surgeon John Watson found himself in need of a home and a roommate, for he had been living in a hotel on the Strand and spending what little money he had more freely than he ought. So alarming did the state of his finances become that he soon realized that he must either leave the metropolis and rusticate somewhere in the country or make a complete alteration to his style of living and take up quarters in some less pretentious and less expensive domicile.

You might say that the roommate gods were smiling on John. Although he had neither kith nor kin in England, he ran into an old acquaintance at the Criterion Bar, who knew just the person.

"Young Stamford told me about Sherlock," he says. "He said that he was a decent enough fellow and an enthusiast in some branches of science—although he had never taken any systematic medical classes and his studies were very desultory and eccentric—and that he was sometimes given to dark moods and was not a man easy to draw out. I was looking for a man of quiet and studious habits, so that all sounded pretty good, although Stamford did say, 'You mustn't blame me if you don't get on with him,' which is probably one of those things people say that you should pay attention to, but whatever.'

The rooms consist of a couple of comfortable bedrooms and a single large, airy sitting room, cheerfully furnished, and illuminated by two broad windows. So desirable in every way were the apartments, and so moderate did the terms seem when divided between them, that the bargain was concluded upon the spot, and they at once entered into possession. That very evening, John moved his things round from the hotel, and on the following morning, Sherlock followed him with several boxes and portmanteaus. For a day or two they were busily employed in unpacking and laying out their property to the best advantage. That done, they gradually began to settle down and to accustom themselves to their new surroundings. Overall, the space has a certain logic to it, admirably balanced, but it is also eccentric and irregular.

"And we have not copied Poe," he says. "So stop saying that."

Of course, bachelor roommates are always learning about each other's habits, but John finds Sherlock "certainly not a difficult man to live with," even with his incredible untidiness, his addiction to music at strange hours, his occasional revolver practice within doors, his weird and often malodorous scientific experiments, and the atmosphere of violence and danger that hangs around him.

"He has a velvet-lined armchair he sits in in the evenings, with the fiddle thrown across his knee," he says. "He plays the violin beautifully, which is lucky because bad violin playing—well, that's not a quality you want in a roommate. The armchair is also a good place to do cocaine and think about your nemesis."

A CHAT WITH JOHN

THEIR STYLE

I never developed much of a taste for the domestic as a soldier, but Sherlock has a rather cavalier style—brusque. Bumptious. With an air of nonchalance. He has high standards. We keep copies of the *Strand* and *Lippincott's* strewn about. We like to sit by the fire and drink port. Sherlock has a taste for French painting. When picking out paintings, he says, "Eliminate all the ugly paintings, and the one that remains, however improbable, must be the one you want to buy."

THEIR INSPIRATION

The city. Urbanity. Sherlock has a variable knowledge of botany. He knows nothing of practical gardening. And we're quite inspired by his work. His cases. I mean, he has *a lot* of disguises, and we have to store all of them somewhere. It is important to keep your disguises organized. You wouldn't want to wear the wrong disguise on the wrong case. An orderly closet is essential.

KEY FEATURES

Our front door makes a big impression. The house number is prominently displayed so visitors think: Oh, yes—this is the house of that crazy guy who solves crimes. We also have some accessories that have been adapted to unconventional uses. Sherlock keeps cigars in the coal scuttle. He also keeps his tobacco in the toe end of his Persian slipper. He smokes a good amount. He doesn't have a curved-stemmed pipe. Maybe I should get him one.

IMPORTANT PIECES

The sofa. During intervals of torpor, he lies upon the sofa in the sitting room, hardly uttering a word or moving a muscle from morning to night. Sometimes in his purple dressing gown. He calls it *the* sofa as it eclipses and predominates the whole of all sofas.

WHAT FRIENDS SAY

We really don't have friends over so much as clients. Mrs. Hudson isn't thrilled that her first-floor flat is invaded at all hours by throngs of singular and often undesirable characters, but she still likes us. And I think she's a very good cook, although Sherlock is a bit pickier.

BIGGEST EMBARRASSMENT

The unanswered letters everywhere. Please stop writing to Sherlock, people.

PROUDEST DIY

Nothing yet, but I think that a wallpapered accent wall behind the sofa would be nice. I like Zoffany's "Dupin," "Lecoq," and "Navarre." I think I'm going to go with "Navarre" in dark chocolate, which is a luxurious large-scale flock design of a dark chocolate fleur-de-lis motif within a trellis pattern on a metallic background which varies in color between aqua and cream, depending on position, lighting, and eyeline. And perhaps a painting of a skull.

BIGGEST CHALLENGE

Our rooms are unique insofar as they serve as both our home and our place of business. Sherlock meets clients in the sitting room. This dual function has posed some design challenges. You want furniture that fits your taste—you don't want the space to say "office" like you're a friggin' clerk or something.

PLANS FOR THE FUTURE

I have been reading about Carlyle's soundproof room, and I think Sherlock would like it. I mentioned it, and he said, "Who's Carlyle?" Anyway. Carlyle does not enjoy street noise: anything from piano-playing neighbors to crowing roosters. "Those cocks must either withdraw or die," he said. So he got double walls, skylights, and a new slated roof with muffling air chambers below. It's the ideal architecture for grouchy men.

BEST ADVICE

Don't be a miserable bungler. Avoid the showy and superficial, and you're sure to have a shrewd approach to your living space.

DECORATING WITH
BARTLEBY THE SCRIVENER

"Wall Street offices are fairly traditional. You aren't going to find beanbags or ping-pong tables. I appreciate a good desk, something with sufficient space for my inkpots and papers. I could say more, but I prefer not to."

E. M. Forster, Howards End

MARGARET AND HELEN'S CULTURED AND SMART CITY HOME

Names: Margaret and Helen Schlegel; no relation to the German guy Coleridge plagiarized

Location: The nice part of London

Size: Large enough for social gatherings of the chattering classes and snug enough to curl up with a good book like *The People of the Abyss*

Years lived in: More than ten; leased (and soon to be pulled down to build new flats—those shitty developers)

THE SOPHISTICATED WICKHAM PLACE is everything one could want in a modern, turn-of-the-century London dwelling for two intelligent and independent women; their dogs, Trilling and Leavis; and their pointless brother, Tibby.

"Tibby is useless. Not just at decorating—at life," says the clear-sighted and selfless Margaret. "At sixteen, he is dyspeptic and difficile and always fancying himself with hay fever. He's not ill-natured, but he is given to do the unwelcome and the unexpected."

But for the Schlegels, the "unexpected" underpins their Continental style, which is infused with a humanizing idealism that contrasts with the wealth-creating energy of the capitalist bourgeoisie. The apartment teems with books, carpets, decorative plates, vases, and busts. A statue of the Angel of Democracy sits on a charming sideboard, and the walls feature a number of tasteful paintings, all hung gallery-style. Tiffany lamps adorn all the rooms, exuding a calming light suited to conversations about whether music has meaning and whether one should be concerned with the plight of the very poor.

"Members of the liberal intelligentsia like throws," she says. "We have a lot of throws. Sometimes I feel bad about the fact that most people do not have as many throws as we do—and this has kept me up on more than one occasion, I confess—but then I think: What can I possibly do about it? It upsets Helen a bit more."

When faced with the staggeringly depressing material inequalities of post-industrial London in the years leading up to the Great War, the Schlegels tend to make tea in their Alessi Michael Graves kettle and book concert tickets. They also love to host. Margaret was fortunate to find an excellent friend in the saintly, kind, and dim Ruth Wilcox, whose intellectually uncurious sexual hypocrite of a husband prefers evenings spent with a newspaper and the empty contents of his conformist bourgeois head.

"The drawing room is an excellent space for the swish of skirts and nonsexual embraces," she says. "We also have a Georgian dining-room table—it's quite traditional, but it suits us. Some people would say to paint it kelly green and pair it with white Eiffel Tower chairs, but that is a bit too modern for us. We are certainly modern—we're very into women's suffrage—but we're just not so into Eiffel Tower chairs."

The apartment is a place to get away from the constant hustle and bustle of the city, where the roads smell of petrol and are difficult to cross, and we human beings hear each other speak with great difficulty, and breathe less of the air, and see less of the sky.

A CHAT WITH MARGARET

THEIR STYLE

I would say that our style is intellectual meets beautiful. We Germans are quite smart and always on the lookout for beauty. We like chrysanthemums and comfortable sofas. We bought a sampler that reads ONLY CONNECT and hung it in a room that is reserved for eating scones and talking about art.

IMPORTANT INFLUENCES

Romantic literature and philosophy. And classical music—lots of Beethoven and absolutely no Wagner. We have six hundred pounds per year each, so we have the thoughts, and things, of six-hundred-pounders. We enjoy eating Elvas plums and discussing the New English Art Club, the dividing line between journalism and literature, and the relative merits of the landscape paintings of Böcklin and Leader. Discussion keeps a house alive. It cannot stand by bricks and mortar alone. Well, it can, obviously—I mean, most people in London live in unconscionable dumps—but that's not our approach.

FAVORITE ELEMENT

Our bookshelves. We have positively tons of them. And bookshelves are not only a great way to communicate to people that you're smart; they're also excellent for murdering people. You just have to knock one over, and blammo! Heart attack. I suggest something tall—like IKEA's Billy bookcases, with the extensions—and you absolutely must *not* anchor them to the wall.

POTENTIAL IMPROVEMENTS

We would love a place in the country. Perhaps an old, redbrick house covered in beautiful vine leaves with a sopping grass lawn for trailing noiselessly over and croquet and calisthenic exercises and meadows where you can collect hay as if you live in a pastoral idyll—a Golden Age, if you will, with lots of silver tea sets. The Wilcoxes have a delightful place where they sit around and talk about golf and motorcars. Dumb-dumbs. Helen spent some time there. The house has red poppies in the garden, dog roses, a very big wych elm with pigs' teeth stuck into the trunk, a paddock for a pony remodeled into a garage, and magnificently tall hedges. I do love a good hedge.

BIGGEST EMBARRASSMENT

Tibby. Without a doubt.

BIGGEST CHALLENGE

Keeping Helen from stealing umbrellas. We keep having to buy new ornate and whimsical umbrella stands to hold all her purloined umbrellas.

BIGGEST INDULGENCE

Meddling in the lives of other people. As with selecting our exotic wallpaper printed with gibbering monkeys, we had the very best of intentions, but good intentions sometimes go wrong.

WHAT FRIENDS SAY

That we women should have the vote. Obvi.

PROUDEST DIY

We haven't done much here at Wickham Place, but we would like to redo our friend Mr. Bast's flat—and his whole sad life, actually. He lives in a neighborhood reeking of metallic fumes, in Block-B flats, in a semibasement, or cellar, which is an amorous and not unpleasant little hole when the curtains are drawn, and the lights turned on, and the gas stove unlit. But it strikes that shallow makeshift note that is so often heard in the modern dwelling place. Come to think of it, his flat resembles a rabbit hutch. His sitting room contains a few chairs, a piano he plays badly and vulgarly, a three-legged table, and a cozy corner. He also has some books by Ruskin and a picture of his buxom, hungry-eyed non-wife, Jacky. So the place could be cheerier.

PLANS FOR THE FUTURE

Maybe put up some portraits of feminists and artists we admire. Dolly Parton comes to mind, obviously. And I'd like to get one of those fridge magnets with that John Waters quote: *If you go home with somebody and they don't have books, don't fuck them.*

DECORATING WITH SOCRATES: CREATING AN IDEAL INTELLECTUAL SPACE

"It would be a good thing if taste in decorating were the sort of thing that flows from the fuller of us into the emptier, just by our touching one another, as the water in wine cups flows through a wool thread from the fuller to the emptier, but we all know this isn't the case. To achieve a Form of Beauty, I suggest a lot of cushions, handsome boys, and wine. Space is extremely important to philosophical debate. I feel extreme *eros* for a comfortable couch where you can recline and engage in dialogues."

Virginia Woolf, Mrs. Dalloway

CLARISSA'S WESTMINSTER PARTY PAD
FOR SAD PARTIES ABOUT DEATH

Names: Clarissa Dalloway, hostess extraordinaire with a touch of the bird about her, and her husband, Richard (so boring—don't worry about him)

Location: London, England

Size: Reasonable

Years lived in: More than twenty; owned

WHEN CLARISSA throws parties in her delightful Westminster home, she buys the flowers and Edible Arrangements herself. Breathing in the sweet, earthy garden smell of the delphiniums, sweet peas, irises, roses, and nodding tufts of lilac at Mulberry's, she feels a wave that she lets flow over her and wash away the sense that eventually she will die and everything will go on without her, and her small life won't amount to a hill of beans in this crazy world.

Clarissa's home has high ceilings, old, tall windows, and a calm atmosphere under which hovers the nagging sense that there must be more to life than this. When she feels plagued by doubts or sadness, she goes shopping on Bond Street.

"I come home with armfuls of parcels of grossly material things," she says. "I suppose we're all just using consumption as a way of dealing with the aching sense of meaninglessness in our postwar moment. And then there was the Spanish flu, too. Which I got. A war and *then* a horrible outbreak of disease? You have got to be kidding me."

Her home has a number of rooms that all look more or less the same. It also boasts a green linoleum bathroom with a dripping tap. Clarissa is always on the lookout for new crystal figurines for the drawing room, a space that has a distinctly aquatic vibe.

"I feel often as I stand hesitating one moment on the threshold of my drawing room, an exquisite suspense, such as might stay a diver before plunging while the sea darkens and brightens beneath him, and the waves which threaten to break, but only gently split their surface, roll and conceal and encrust as they just turn over the weeds with pearl," she says. "Of course, there aren't any actual weeds in the room, which is good. I just wish I had learned how to scuba dive."

Clarissa loves Shakespeare and has several collections of his poetry and plays. Richard is unlikely to be found looking over this bookshelf as he shuns all expressions of authentic emotion as foolish.

"Richard asks me how I can swallow that stuff about poetry. He says that no decent man ought to read Shakespeare's sonnets because it's like listening at keyholes. I guess he means that it's like spying on people's, um, intimacies. We don't have any keyholes in our house. Or intimacies."

Beloved by her servants, Clarissa also strives to be a carefree and relaxed hostess. This is important as she is defined by her social roles and not by her own ineffable self.

"You don't want to work yourself into a tizzy before a party," she says. "You need to be cool and collected so you can make small talk with all your empty-headed friends."

Clarissa's bedroom is a retreat from her responsibilities as the perfect hostess, as well as from the hustle and bustle of London's streets. One of the room's best features is a dressing table, where she removes the hairpins from her hair and has overpowering ecstatic memories of her "friend" Sally Seton, who was way better than dull-as-paint Richard. Had not that, after all, been love?

Anyway. The room is also adorned with a half-burnt candle and a narrow bed with clean, tightly stretched sheets. Although it is a room of her own, it is pretty depressing.

"A virginity preserved through childbirth clings to me like a sheet," she says. "You can't buy that from Frette."

A CHAT WITH CLARISSA

HER STYLE

"Politician's wife." That's how your home is supposed to look if you're some-one like me. A mistress always knows the temper of her house. You want a home where men can talk about laws and women can talk about dresses and paying calls. I'm drawn to design that is repressive. Wait—*restrained*! I meant to say restrained! Bit of a slip there!

IMPORTANT INFLUENCES

Westminster Abbey. Westminster Cathedral. The palace of Westminster. I want the house to really be a Westminster house. Safe. Like everyone else. If you incorporate any surprising elements, your sheeplike friends will not be able to handle it.

IMPORTANT PIECES

I like trays. Giant candlesticks. The silver casket on the mantelpiece. My lovely inlaid table. My crystal dolphin. It's a classy crystal dolphin—not from Hallmark or anything like that. I am the mistress of silver, of linen, of china. Sometimes I wonder what it would be like to have a job.

INTERESTING FEATURES

There is an open staircase window from which I can hear dogs barking and the grinding, blowing, flowering of the day. What a lark! What a plunge! You know, maybe if I got a dog, I would feel like my life had more of a purpose. I would need to walk it and feed it and talk to it, perhaps about the war and all the shell-shocked returned soldiers, or about the popular fashions for those of us who are amazingly still alive. Dogs like it when you talk to them.

WHAT FRIENDS SAY

Peter says that the house is exactly what he would expect: bougie like I am. But he wanted to marry me and I rejected him, so he is hardly objective. He used to say that my taste was sentimental. Now he writes dull letters and fiddles around with his pocketknife. He really needs to quit it with the goddamn pocketknife.

BIGGEST SPLURGE

I have a stone urn with flowers in it that is molded on one at Bourton, where I spent time when I was younger and hadn't yet made all the sensible decisions that closed down any kinds of real possibility in my life. Bourton had French windows that squeaked when they opened, blinds that used to flap, and a terrace in the moonlight. I spent my days wandering around in white dresses, kissing Sally Seton, and drinking Pimm's. Sometimes the urn makes me nostalgic for my lost youth, and sometimes it makes me think that my life is rather ordinary, and sometimes I just think it is pretty.

BIGGEST EMBARRASSMENT

That the Bradshaws talked of death at my party. What business had they to talk of death at my party? A young man had killed himself. And they talked of it at my party. Not okay. There are some topics that are appropriate at a party, including your kitchen remodeling, your recent resort vacations, and where your precious children are going to college. Talking about soldiers flinging themselves out of windows and impaling themselves on railings— that is not polite conversation. And as a hostess, I don't have time to feel inexplicably connected to dead strangers. I need to be sure that my guests are getting drunk enough to forget how boring they are.

BEST ADVICE

Look below the surface of things when you're planning a room. Some things look quite conventional, but they actually have these massively complex inner lives that no one can see. Yep.

Tennessee Williams, A Streetcar Named Desire

STELLA AND STANLEY'S NOT OVERLY WELCOMING NEW ORLEANS WALK-UP

Names: Stanley Kowalski, a ruggedly masculine man of Polish descent with a deep knowledge of the Napoleonic code; his wife, Stella, a gentle young woman of a background obviously quite different from her husband's; and mothlike visiting sister, Blanche

Location: New Orleans, Louisiana (the old part of town; take the streetcar named Desire and then transfer to the one called Cemeteries)

Size: Not big enough for three, that's for sure

Years lived in: It's hard to know when you're having this much sex; rented

WHEN NEWLYWEDS Stella and Stanley set up in their simple but raffishly charming old New Orleans flat, they had no idea that they would soon have a houseguest. Located in a two-story corner building on a street named Elysian Fields (come on) and known for the interminable "blue piano" music emanating from a nearby bar, their snug two-room apartment is not too cheerily defined but is suited to their pared-down approach to domesticity. Stella was happy to "downsize" from her ancestral estate, Belle Reve, a great big place with white columns that was lost for reasons Stanley would really like to know a whole lot more about.

"My sister says that you don't need a fancy estate to be happy if you have a really manly man," says fallen Southern belle Blanche, touching her handkerchief to her forehead. "She's a great sister, and I know I can always depend on her."

Blanche sleeps in a folding bed in the kitchen, which sometimes has a raw, lurid atmosphere—as on Stanley's poker nights (the game is seven-card stud)—but at other times, it is aglow with summer brilliance. The room beyond the kitchen is the bedroom, where Stella and Stanley shack up. The kitchen has a screen door that Stanley likes to throw open in an annoyingly animalistic manner, as well as a yellow-checked linoleum table and a chair in which Blanche can sit and listen to screeching cats. The chair is perfectly situated to allow for a view of the half-opened closet, where Stanley hides the whiskey that Blanche secretly drinks.

"One's my limit," she says with feverish vivacity. "I haven't turned into a drunkard. Certainly not! It's just my nerves. Fiddle-dee-dee!"

The building itself oozes old New Orleans charm. The houses in the neighborhood are mostly white frame, weathered gray, with rickety outside stairs and galleries and quaintly ornamented gables. The sky is a peculiarly tender blue, almost a turquoise, which invests the scene with a kind of lyricism and gracefully attenuates the atmosphere of decay. You can almost feel the warm breath of the brown river beyond the river warehouses with their faint redolences of bananas and coffee, but you can't actually because it would be weird if a river breathed. Stanley and Stella's building contains two flats, upstairs and down, with faded white stairs that ascend to the entrances of both. The courtyard is a delightful place to sit and drink a lemon-coke on a sultry evening or to cry out your wife's name in a state of drunken and dejected misery.

"Stanley is unrefined," says Blanche. "Like this shithole."

A CHAT WITH BLANCHE

HER STYLE

Far more chic than this place. I would say my style is "Virgin-Whore," with an element of magic. I like lace, feathers, fur, gold, things that sparkle, costumey things—Hollywood glamour stuff, as Stanley says. My style is really embodied in my trunk, which contains all the papers about our lost estate, as well as a number of lovely gifts I received from admirers. Stanley likes to rummage through it and throw things all over the place because he thinks he's going to find some sort of clue as to what really happened to Belle Reve. Well, I can tell you what happened to Belle Reve. What happened were epic fornications. Yep, the four-letter word. My dude relatives boned the place away.

HER INSPIRATION

My style is very "plantation," which just means beautiful and rich and lady-like and has nothing to do with anything else in the history of the South. But that's not Stella's style. I would say that her apartment is inspired by Edgar Allan Poe, but without a dismembered body under the floorboards. I told Stella that the place was horrible, and I think I might have hurt her feelings. I meant to say something nice about it. But sometimes I get the sense that I'm not welcome, like Stanley is threatened by me in some fundamental way that has to do with class and gender, but I'm probably just being silly.

FAVORITE ELEMENT

The bathtub is a great relief for my nerves. I can soak in there forever, even in this hot weather. And the bathroom is quiet and private. I'm very into privacy. God, I don't know why I'm telling you that! Scratch that. It's private. None of your business! A lady doesn't reveal her private things. Now leave me alone so I can *absolutely not* have a drink.

MOST MENACING FEATURE

Sometimes polka music rises up, faint in the distance, and that is kind of stressful. And the apartment could have a better lighting scheme. Maybe put everything on a dimmer. I hate overhead lights. I won't be looked at

in a merciless glare! My delicate beauty must avoid a strong light. I found a paper lantern for the naked lightbulb, and Stanley's friend Mitch helped me put it up. He has a dead ex, too. How crazy a coincidence is that? We have so much in common. But anyway, can you imagine a lightbulb just shining like that, uncovered, lighting up the whole place? I would prefer that we just turn off all the lights on the planet, but that seems like a hard thing to do, so I just got the lantern.

WHAT FRIENDS SAY

Let me see. A young man came by one evening, and he liked my long gossamer scarf, and I said that he looked like a prince out of the *Arabian Nights* and called him a "honey lamb," and then maybe I said and did some other stuff, and then he got uncomfortable and left.

BIGGEST EMBARRASSMENT

Well, Stella and Stanley's room is just *right there*, and I don't like to say it, but their relationship strikes me as rather—well. He is so coarse and direct and powerful. Suffice to say that when I arrived, I didn't know where Stella was going to put me. I was worried it wouldn't be decent, with me sleeping there in the kitchen, with just those curtains between us. I don't want to think about what sorts of things go on in there, but I know it's a lot of boning.

PROUDEST DIY

I re-covered the chair with diagonal green and white stripes, so now it is an even better chair for sitting in a tense, hunched position. And once I lit a candle and put it in a bottle to create a bohemian Left-Bank-of-Paris atmosphere—as though I were in an artist's café and not trapped in this hellhole.

BIGGEST INDULGENCE

Stella and I try to carve out some space for ourselves, which is hard in such a masculine space. Sometimes we go out, just to get away from it all. Stanley isn't the easiest roommate. He likes cards and bowling and yelling. And drinking. And sweating. And crying.

BEST ADVICE

Some jasmine perfume will spruce up a room. Even if the room is really a prison of your own fantasies and delusions.

PLANS FOR THE FUTURE

I plan to trade out this cramped apartment for a cruise in the Caribbean. Mr. Shep Huntleigh of Dallas and I are going to the tropics. Doesn't that sound nice? I will wear my somewhat soiled and crumpled white satin evening gown and a pair of scuffed silver slippers with brilliants set in their heels. He'll be here any minute. I wish that woman outside would shut up about the flowers for the dead. No dead people here, lady! You must have me confused with someone else. God, these walls are so damn thin.

HOW TO PRESERVE YOUR LONG-DEAD LOVE INTEREST IN A ROSE-COLORED VAGINA ROOM WITH MISS EMILY GRIERSON

"My house is a big, squarish frame house that was once white, decorated with cupolas and spires and scrolled balconies in the heavily lightsome style of the eighteen-seventies, set on what was once the most select street in Jefferson, Mississippi. That's in Yoknapatawpha County, if you're not familiar. Now the place is known for its stubborn and coquettish decay—some call it an 'eyesore among eyesores'—but the interior is rather surprising. I'm speaking, of course, about the room in that region abovestairs. I decked and furnished it as for a bride: the valance curtains of faded rose color, the rose-shaded lights, the dressing table, the delicate array of crystal and the man's toilet things backed with tarnished silver, silver so tarnished that the monogram was obscured. And then of course there is the man in the bed. Homer Barron. He makes a lovely addition to the space, with his profound and fleshless grin. You definitely want some patient and abiding dust in a room like this. And don't forget a long strand of your iron-gray hair next to the corpse. The hair is absolutely key to your necrophiliac aesthetic."

INTERLUDE:
OUTSIDER DOMICILES

Love, family, friends, and fellowship are all well and good, but sometimes you find yourself living on the outskirts of society. For former monarch and not-great houseguest King Lear, a hovel on a blasted heath provides much-needed shelter from the pelting of a pitiless storm. And for Southern recluse Boo Radley, a crumbling house shields him from meddling neighbors, curious children, and the terrible one-horse town in which he lives.

KING LEAR: As a major tragic figure, I'm bound to have moments of recognition—what Aristotle called *anagnorisis*, if you will—

BOO RADLEY: I will.

KING LEAR: —and there just came a point in my life when I realized that I didn't need so much stuff. I suppose this was sometime after I brutally rejected my youngest daughter and then was kicked out of the house of my eldest.

BOO RADLEY: We really do allow ourselves to be weighed down by material objects. Experiences are what matter in life, not possessions. We could all live so much more simply.

KING LEAR: Precisely. Take your average castle. You have thrones and scepters and crowns and maps and all sorts of things that just take up so much space. But houseless poverty: Now that is really something. Unaccommodated man.

BOO RADLEY: No clutter.

KING LEAR: If you live in clutter, your mind is bound to be cluttered, too.

BOO RADLEY: Right. This is why I don't have screen doors. Clutter.

KING LEAR: Yes.

BOO RADLEY: And people take up space in a house. Best not to have any of them.

KING LEAR: Right. That's why I systematically destroyed all my relationships.

BOO RADLEY: For me, turning away from the social pressures to live in a particular way was so important. I just wanted to do my own thing. Have my own Grey Gardens, if you will.

KING LEAR: I will.

BOO RADLEY: A property that some refer to as "droopy and sick."

KING LEAR: I have found my hovel on the heath to be more than comfortable. I can just duck in there if I'm tired.

BOO RADLEY: Yes.

KING LEAR: Or if the tyranny of the open night's too rough for nature to endure. Which is to say, if it's raining.

BOO RADLEY: Or if you're worried that you're going mad.

KING LEAR: That, too. And it's large enough for my fool, who is constantly reminding me about my extremely poor life choices.

BOO RADLEY: I find it's best to just never leave my house at all. I mean, what for? I have everything I need here. A rocking chair. Windows—with good shutters on them—for peering out onto the cruel world that has rejected me.

KING LEAR: We're really very avant-garde, when you think about it. This is exactly the way I wanted my life to go. And I think I have some great things to look forward to in the future.

BOO RADLEY: Well, that's unlikely, as you're in a tragedy.

KING LEAR: I suppose it's best not to think about the future anyway. Live in the present, that's what I say.

BOO RADLEY: And set up a place for yourself that is suited to your utter lack of interest in that desperately flawed thing we refer to as humanity. You know what they call me? A *malevolent phantom*. Fine. Whatever, kids.

KING LEAR: That is really unaccounted for.

BOO RADLEY: These small-town people. When people's azaleas froze in a cold snap, everyone said it was because I had breathed on them.

KING LEAR: Unreal. My terrible daughter Goneril said—

BOO RADLEY: And when people's chickens and household pets were found mutilated, of course that was my fault, too. It turned out that the culprit was Crazy Addie, who eventually drowned himself in Barker's Eddy. And apparently the pecans that grow on my tree will kill you. Let's just say that I don't think I'm missing out on much by not knowing these people.

KING LEAR: And I totally don't miss having a family. At all. I'm doing great in my hovel.

BOO RADLEY: We have what we need. My kitchen is simple, but it's a perfect place to dine on the raw squirrels and cats that everyone says I eat.

KING LEAR: Everyone does say that.

BOO RADLEY: And there's no reason to be overly fastidious about maintenance. My house was once white with a deep front porch and green shutters, but it has darkened to the color of the slate-gray yard around it. Rain-rotted shingles droop over the eaves of the veranda; oak trees keep the sun away. Sun is the worst.

KING LEAR: My hovel is extremely easy to maintain. I just ask my fool to even out the dirt floor from time to time, and then he makes jokes that I don't understand.

BOO RADLEY: It's okay for an outsider domicile to be a bit weathered. You might have a pile of old, rusted metal on your property, but if you add some more rusted metal, you have an instant update.

KING LEAR: Or you could add another rock. Maybe something you picked up when you were out raging against the storm.

BOO RADLEY: People really are the worst.

KING LEAR: They are. I am a man more sinned against than sinning.

BOO RADLEY: I'm not entirely convinced of that, buddy.

IV.

FAMILY
PADS

L. Frank Baum, The Wonderful Wizard of Oz

DOROTHY'S CYCLONE-PLAGUED PRAIRIE FARMHOUSE

Names: Dorothy; Aunt Em, who washes dishes and never smiles; and Uncle Henry, a man who never laughs and does not know what joy is

Location: Kansas, in the very flat part, way out past the other flat part

Size: Small, as the lumber to build it had to be carried by wagon many miles across the flat part and into the very flat part

Years lived in: A while (When Aunt Em came there to live, she was a young, pretty wife, but the sun and wind have changed her and taken the sparkle from her eyes and left them a sober gray; try one afternoon of being a prairie wife and see how it goes for you); owned

FOR ANYONE WHO has ever wanted to get away from it all, a Kansas prairie farmhouse is just the ticket. Dorothy is fortunate to live in the midst of these great prairies with her hardworking, silent farmer uncle and his equally somber wife. The one-room house has an almost prefab minimalism to it, with its four walls, floor, and roof. This all-purpose room contains a rusty-looking cooking stove, a cupboard for dishes, a table, three or four chairs, and the beds. Uncle Henry and Aunt Em have a big bed in one corner and Dorothy a little bed in another corner.

"It's like a studio apartment, but you have two sad and life-wearied roommates, and you live in the middle of nowhere," says Dorothy.

The property also has some sheds where the cows and horses are kept, but they are just normal cows and horses and not Kalidahs, which have bodies like bears and heads like tigers and are not a thing in Kansas.

Location is everything when constructing a farmhouse, and the flatness and grayness of the Kansas prairie ideally complement the house's simplicity. When Dorothy stands in the doorway and looks around, she can see nothing but the great gray prairie on every side. Not a tree nor a house breaks the broad sweep of flat country that reaches to the edge of the sky in all directions. The sun has baked the ploughed land into a gray mass, with little cracks running through it. Even the grass is not green, for the sun has burned the tops of the long blades until they are the same gray color to be seen everywhere. So that's the deal with prairies.

Uncle Henry and Aunt Em also found inspiration in the prairie's grayness when selecting the exterior paint. They wanted a color that would be blistered by the sun and washed away by the rain, as that is what happens in Kansas.

"Now the color is as dull and gray as everything else," says Dorothy. "They probably should have gone with a durable, all-weather laminate siding. But, you know, hindsight and twenty-twenty and all that."

There is no garret at all, and no cellar, but the house does boast a small hole, dug in the ground, called a cyclone cellar, where the family can go in case a great whirlwind arises, mighty enough to crush any building in its path. The cyclone cellar is reached by a trapdoor in the middle of the floor, from which a ladder leads down into the small, dark space.

"Cyclone cellars are the sort of thing preppers are into," says Dorothy. "They stockpile water, canned food, generators, flashlights, and stuff like that for when the apocalypse happens. But that's not the way we think about it. I'm not convinced the apocalypse is coming. Aunt Em and Uncle Henry say that life is just steady, unchanging, and routine and stretches out for miles and miles until the end."

A CHAT WITH DOROTHY

THEIR STYLE

All-American, I would say. Very much inspired by the plains. We like things that are flat. Tables, floors, tops of dressers. Uncle Henry had to rebuild the farmhouse after the old one was blown away in a cyclone. But this one is pretty much the same as the other one. We're people of habit; keep it simple, I always say (#KeepItSimple). No frilly curtains and knickknacks like you see in some farmhouses. Aunt Em likes her cabbages. I like anything that says: There's no place like home. I'm very invested in my home, both as an actual place and, you might say, as an idea.

THEIR INSPIRATION

Beauty. Beautiful things are good, and ugly things are bad. That's how it works with witches and houses. So I look for beautiful things. I saw some interesting mouse houses in this dream I had about the Land of Oz. And I stayed in a green emerald palace with a comfortable bed that had sheets of green silk and a green velvet counterpane, and a tiny fountain in the middle of the room that shot a spray of green perfume into the air, and books filled with green pictures. It was beautiful, but I do think you want to mix up your color palette. All that emerald is a bit much.

IMPORTANT INFLUENCES

Well, in this dream I also saw a country of china people with china houses painted in the brightest colors. There were also pretty little china barns, with fences around them, and horses and pigs and chickens made of china, and a china milkmaid milking a china cow. I think we could learn from their attention to detail, but Aunt Em just said what's the point and screw the American Dream and you work and work and are never any better off than you were before.

FAVORITE ELEMENT

We have some reclaimed barnwood shelves on which we have displayed the dishes that Aunt Em spends her whole allotted time on earth washing. And the doorstep is nice. Uncle Henry sits there, with his long beard and his rough boots, looking anxiously at the sky.

WHAT FRIENDS SAY

That we should put shiplap in one of the rooms—or I guess I mean in the one room. I blame *Fixer Upper* for people's obsession with shiplap. We'd like to work on the garden and maybe add some color to the relentless palette of gray. I suggested poppies, but they may not be ideal as they can kill you.

BIGGEST EMBARRASSMENT

I crushed a witch with my old house, but it was okay because she was wicked and ugly. When we had the terrible cyclone, I went down to the cellar with my dog, Toto, and then a strange thing happened and the house whirled around and rose through the air, and before I knew it, *BANG*. Dead witch. This witch's sister had a palace with a lot of crows and scary monkeys. But crows and scary monkeys are too over-the-top for me, décor-wise.

IMPORTANT FEATURE

Our crops. Crops really make a farmhouse. They were pretty crappy last year, and Uncle Henry says if things aren't better this year, we're not going to be able to afford anything, not even a single panel of stupid shiplap.

PROUDEST DIY

Sometimes if I have a moment, I arrange some wheat in a vase. But we don't have time for DIY as we work from morning to evening without rest. Toto is a great relief, given the relentless repetitiveness of life. He is my little black dog, and he plays all day long and has long silky hair and small black eyes that twinkle merrily on either side of his funny, wee nose. He makes me laugh, but Aunt Em and Uncle Henry find this laughing sound confusing, so I try not to do it too often.

BIGGEST CHALLENGE

We don't really have any closets, but that's not the end of the world as I just own one light-blue-and-white gingham dress, a white blouse, two ribbons for my hair, and a picnic basket. In this dream I was telling you about, I had the most amazing silver shoes: the kind of thing you would get from Irregular Choice. Except they were given to me by a beautiful, good witch. I would have preferred ruby red, but silver was good, too.

PLANS FOR THE FUTURE

I'd love to bring in some details from Munchkin Country, another place in my dream. When the cyclone set down my house there very gently, I got to see all the marvelous beauty: fruits and flowers and birds with rare and brilliant plumage, and a small brook rushing and sparkling along green banks. The Munchkins' houses are round with domed roofs, and then, of course, there is the Yellow Brick Road. It's an entirely different color scheme than here. And I would like to have a nice oil portrait commissioned of Toto. But maybe we'll just put in a sliding barn door in a nice knotty pine? After all, a farmhouse has to have a sliding barn door.

LOVING YOUR HOME WITH MY ÁNTONIA

"My farm is rather bohemian. Romantic. It looks like a sepia-toned photograph or the album cover of Springsteen's *Nebraska*. Land is important to me. And light. It's important to harness light in a house—not just actual light but also the light of God that supports Manifest Destiny."

P. L. Travers, Mary Poppins

GEORGE AND WINIFRED'S ENCHANTED EDWARDIAN EDIFICE

Names: George Banks, corporate stooge fond of red carnation boutonnieres; his put-upon wife, Winifred; and their children, Jane and Michael (and twins John and Barbara, but no one knows about them because they weren't in the movie)

Location: Number Seventeen Cherry-Tree Lane, London, England (where the houses run down one side and the Park runs down the other and the cherry trees go dancing right down the middle)

Size: Smallest house in the Lane

Years lived in: Since George decided to buy it; owned

IF YOU WANT TO FIND Cherry-Tree Lane all you have to do is ask the Policeman at the crossroads. He will push his helmet slightly to one side, scratch his head thoughtfully, and then he will point his huge white-gloved finger and say: "First to your right, second to your left, sharp right again, and you're there. Good-morning." Because policemen in an enormous urban metropolis always know where everyone lives.

It's a nice little spot, you might say.

The house is rather dilapidated and needs a coat of paint, but there is a perfectly reasonable explanation for this. In selecting a house, George told Winifred that she must consider their future family. He explained that she could have either a nice, clean, comfortable house or four children. But not both, for he couldn't afford it. Aware that her highest duty was to reproduce, Winifred chose the latter. They have a pleasant drawing room in the Victorian style, where Winifred writes letters all day and wonders what you might call this system in which her husband makes all the money and decisions.

What Number Seventeen lacks in elegance, it makes up for in hired help. Mrs. Brill cooks for the family, Ellen lays the table, and Robertson Ay cuts the lawn, cleans the knives, and polishes the shoes, while George resents the fact that he has to pay him for this labor. Their former nanny, Katie Nanna, recently quit, but she was promptly replaced by a mean witch named Mary Poppins who showed up with a talking parrot-head umbrella and a magic carpet bag. Up the street are Miss Annie and Miss Fannie, who stand on a ladder and glue gingerbread stars to the sky. As one does.

George's taste runs to the corporate. In "the City," he sits in a large chair in front of a large desk and makes money. He also has a strange interest in which way the wind is blowing. To determine this, he relies on a telescope located on a nearby property: the grandest house on the Lane, at the corner, which is owned by Admiral Boom. The Admiral's house is built exactly like a ship, with a flagstaff in the garden and a gilt weathercock shaped like a telescope on the roof. It's really not clear what happened to the Admiral at sea.

Mary Poppins's signature piece is a mirror as she has a hard time wrenching herself away from her glorious reflection. The children's taste in décor runs to windows, and the house has a number of these, in which they sit and wait for their father to return from his daily capitulation to the machine of capitalism that robs him of any real creative or emotional life and traps him in a model of masculinity that does not make him happy.

A CHAT WITH WINIFRED

HER STYLE

Edwardian décor is rather ornate, and it makes my heart go pitter-patter with excitement. I like rich woods—oak and walnut and lots of mahogany. You can never have too many things in mahogany. I like the curved

shapes and cabriole legs of Queen Anne furniture, but George says I'm not allowed to buy anything. George has a nice umbrella stand in the hall, next to which he keeps his bag for work. Sometimes he accidentally leaves it in his study when he's working on income tax papers, and then he blames us and lectures us about how the bag must always be kept in one place. You know, I knew this really nice, bookish man named Fred when I was younger. I don't know why I'm thinking about that now! I wonder if he's on Facebook.

IMPORTANT INFLUENCES

The nursery is the most important room as that's where we keep the children quarantined. There, I would say the influence has been the supernatural, thanks to our new employee, Mary Poppins. There are lots of toys, which Mary Poppins cleans up magically and effortlessly because that's how labor works.

INTERESTING FEATURES

We have some decorative vases that we have to rescue from breaking when the Admiral fires his cannon. And a dark and gloomy chimney that occasionally needs sweeping by Dick Van Dyke, who will eventually apologize for his atrocious Cockney accent. Let's see. What else? We have a stuffed pigeon to remind the children of the Bird Woman at St. Paul's. She calls out, "Feed the birds, tuppence a bag!" and all round her fly the birds, circling and leaping and swooping and rising, and swarming upon the food, pushing and scrambling and shouting. They sit all over her—on her shoulders, knees, and hat, and at night she spreads out her skirt, and the birds go creep, creep, creeping underneath, and she settles down over them, making little brooding, nesting noises. I thought that if we got this decorative bird, the kids would stop asking to go see this lady.

HER INSPIRATION

Order. George runs his home precisely on schedule. At 6:01, he marches through his door. His slippers, sherry, and pipe are due at 6:02. Consistent is the life he leads. All the chaos stays in the nursery and in Mary Poppins's room. She says that her room is quite suitable. It has a simple iron bed and a bureau, and she brought her own hatstand, potted plant, lamp, and large gold mirror because she travels with furniture.

IMPORTANT PIECES

There is a mantelpiece in the nursery, where Mary Poppins keeps her bottle of dark crimson medicine. Children need to be drugged to sleep, you know. There's also a lovely clock on the mantelpiece, which ticks out the time until Jane and Michael's inevitable abandonment by their weird flying nurse.

KEY FEATURES

George has a study, where Ellen dusts the books on his bureau bookcase. All the books are about money. He says that it's a waste of time to read books about anything else. He has a desk with an inkpot, pen, and blotter, and sometimes he works in his study after dinner so he doesn't have to spend time with us.

BIGGEST SPLURGE

I bought a set of *Votes for Women* dinner plates, side plates, and mugs that reminds me of the times I have been clapped in irons. Sometimes I march around the house in my sash and sing about how our daughters' daughters will adore us and will sing in grateful chorus: *Well done, sister suffragette!* As I always say, though we adore men individually, we agree that as a group they're rather stupid. Thus the dishes.

WHAT FRIENDS SAY

Uncle Albert thinks the house is a bit dull, but he doesn't know anything about design. He spends his time floating in the air, filled up with laughing gas like a balloon. He doesn't even require a chair. Anyway, I think that floating furniture would be dangerous. But we all have *that* uncle.

BIGGEST CHALLENGE

Probably all the house envy on our block. Miss Lark lives next door in a wonderful house with a garden and two gates—one for her friends and the other for the butcher and the baker and the milkman—and the Admiral is rather jealous of it. (Her very posh dog, Andrew, sleeps on a silk pillow.) When he rolls past it he says, "Blast my gizzard! What does *she* want with a house like that?" He means that women who live alone don't deserve any space because they have failed to marry.

PLANS FOR THE FUTURE

I'd like to try to get Michael to behave. Mrs. Brill and Ellen sit in the kitchen and drink strong cups of tea all day, and sometimes he goes in there and kicks Mrs. Brill in the legs when she won't let him eat the leftover scone batter, and then he says she deserves it because she is fat. So I think it's pretty clear he's going to turn out like his father.

DECORATING WITH PETER PAN

"We wanted Wendy to have a house in Neverland where she could pretend to be our mother— even though she is just a child—and cook for us and darn our stockings. Because I'm an excellent architect, I measured her with my feet to see how large a house she would need. She sang a song about wanting a pretty house with funny little red walls and a roof of mossy green and gay windows all about and roses peeping in and babies peeping out. But this was a little greedy, I think. Maybe that's why Tinker Bell *hates* her."

THE MARCHES' MASSACHUSETTS WOMAN CAVE

Names: Stalwart mother, Marmee, and her daughters, Jo, Beth, Meg, and Amy

Location: Concord, Massachusetts

Size: Tasteful and modest, with a twelve-acre apple orchard

Years lived in: Their whole happy and fulfilled, but also challenging, lives; owned

BEAUTIFUL IN EVERY SEASON, the March family's two-story clapboard farmhouse is sturdy and spartan, with unique details like wide-plank pine floors.

"Thank god some idiot didn't put down wall-to-wall carpet," says Jo, who likes reading books, speaking her mind, climbing trees, and lying on the rug and grumbling that Christmas won't be Christmas without any presents. She also likes fires but says that you should not stand too close to them or you will burn your frock, and then your family will be embarrassed.

The house has a distinctly self-sustaining, feminine vibe, but for rebellious and tomboyish Jo, femininity can conflict with creativity and artistic freedom. In decorating.

"Propriety isn't everything," says Jo. "To be truly creative—beyond IKEA Hackers creative—you have to enter a kind of trancelike state. A vortex, if you will."

Amy is sweet and pretty and paints the kinds of pictures that you buy to match your sofa. Meg wants nothing more than to be a wife to a kind and rather dull man and mother to his children. And Beth likes puppies and rainbows and talking about how she doesn't want or need anything. The family spends much of their time in the kitchen, parlor, and dining room. Their father spends much of his time at war, where he may be killed or maimed at any moment. But Marmee buoys her daughters' spirits by going on and on about happiness and goodness, making rag rugs, and canning things.

"Even at the end of a taxing day of charity work, Marmee still has absolutely bottomless emotional energy for us all," says Jo. "Our dining room is where we really come together in the evenings. You want a space suited to good table talk. We discuss abolitionism and social reform and apples."

As these are hard times, the Marches live economically, but they try to budget in a way that allows for the occasional festive family dinner—champagne living on a beer budget, you might say, but Jo notes, "We don't drink." The family treasures paintings of churches, handmade quilts, and anything with an adage on it (#PutAnAdageOnIt). In the parlor, details such as portraits, dolls, and books by Nathaniel Hawthorne (a very quiet guy) make for a snug atmosphere. In the kitchen, a farmhouse hutch displays china, chipped enamelware, and a surprising number of stoneware butter crocks.

"We like to unwind in the kitchen after a long day of trying to contribute meaningfully to society," says Jo. "Our loyal servant Hannah also loves the kitchen. It doesn't have an island, but it's quite adequate, with a nice array of mortars and pestles and some wooden bowls that you can put things in, like batter or apples."

A CHAT WITH JO

HER STYLE

Simple and cheerful. We like things that create a pleasant atmosphere of home peace. Our rooms are comfortable and old, with faded carpets and plain furniture and a good picture or two hanging on the walls. We have a hearth where Beth can warm her slippers. Our home is the perfect place to put on plays, knit in the twilight, and write our mock-Dickensian newspaper. Of course, I would prefer more of an element of sentiment, fairy tale, and melodrama. Something a bit more sensationalist. Maybe a crystal

chandelier worthy of a great romance. But not like Plumfield, which is so gaudy, and not like next door, although I don't really know what that place looks like inside as Mr. Laurence keeps Laurie locked up like an effing prisoner, curtains down at the little windows and everything.

IMPORTANT INFLUENCES

Transcendentalism, but of course I like to think that our approach constitutes a feminist critique. Thoreau is so independent and self-sufficient, with help from his mother. Think of his cabin. You might say that he decorated deliberately, that he sucked out all the marrow of life—and also that his mom brought him cookies and did his laundry.

FAVORITE ELEMENT

Our grandfather clock reminds you of each passing day and exhorts you to lead a meaningful and thoughtful life. Everyone should have a grandfather clock—I mean, if they can afford one and aren't living in a shack in the woods like the poor Hummels, with a baby dying of scarlet fever. Then a grandfather clock seems like less of a priority.

BEST FEATURE

Nothing jumps to mind. Honestly, I love our house, but I'm just dying to go to New York. I know that living in a boardinghouse wouldn't be very glamorous, but to be in the big city! Keep your woods, O Nature, and the quiet places by the woods. Give me faces and streets! Give me these phantoms incessant and endless along the trottoirs! Give me the streets of Manhattan! Whew—sorry. I got a bit carried away there.

WHAT FRIENDS SAY

Simone de Beauvoir likes the fact that I hate housekeeping and sewing, and she really knows what she's talking about.

BIGGEST EMBARRASSMENT

Amy wanted to paint the parlor this awful lime color because she was *obsessed* with limes. We told her absolutely not. And Meg went to a party at the Moffats', and then she was upset that our house isn't as splendid and elegant as theirs. They're rich idiots, and eventually Meg figured that out because Laurie explained it to her. She had let that empty-headed fool Annie dress her up like a doll with fuss and feathers and rouge. The vanity of it! Sometimes I have the feeling that we're all being tested in a sort of allegorical way, almost like a journey or a progress, but I'm probably just being paranoid.

PROUDEST DIY

War makes you very crafty. We make a lot of bandages for the soldiers. It's important for women to support men in times of war by doing things like sitting by the fire and rolling up fabric and reflecting on the value of heroism. The bandages are a gorgeous gauze that would also work well for a range of crafts. I could see us making some decorative roses to hang in the entryway, but for now, they're really just to soak up the blood of dying men.

BIGGEST INDULGENCE

My books. Books really make a home. Shakespeare, Goethe, all the big male geniuses that we women feel compelled to measure ourselves against. That, and my "mood pillow." When it's placed upright on the couch, it means that I'm happy. But when the pillow is on its side, everyone had better beware, for I might be in one of my "moods," which is a word we use for what women are like when they are thinking.

PLANS FOR THE FUTURE

I'm not marrying Laurie, that's for sure.

MARILLA AND MATTHEW'S GOD-FEARING
AVONLEA ORPHAN SANCTUARY

Names: Marilla and Matthew Cuthbert, bickering but affectionate siblings d'un certain âge

Location: Prince Edward Island, Canada, past Barry's Pond (or the Lake of Shining Waters) and down the Avenue (or the White Way of Delight)

Size: Appropriate and sensible

Years lived in: Since their youth, which was spent nursing their dying father rather than courting; owned

WHEN MATTHEW AND MARILLA decided to adopt a little orphan boy from the asylum in Nova Scotia, they had no idea what was in store, nor did the word "asylum" strike them as a problem. Although Mrs. Rachel Lynde was certain that the child would murder them in their beds and burn the place to the ground, the alternative was to hire a local French boy, and French boys are incredibly stupid. Due to a queer mistake, the Cuthberts received a girl, Anne, who was next door to a perfect heathen but really pretty great. Sometimes home improvements go hand in hand with Providence, and the adoption of this skinny and homely girl led to a total reimagining of the bachelor and old maid's farmhouse.

Green Gables has a hollow, a brook, white birches, horizon mists of pearl and purple, and other things of that manner. It is one of the finest properties in Avonlea, a peaceful and God-fearing place where the most anticipated social event of the year is a teetotaling afternoon party at the manse. The farm is surrounded by cherry- and apple-tree orchards that shower the landscape with blossoms, and the grass is all sprinkled with dandelions. Rose bushes give way to green, low-sloping fields that offer a sparkling blue glimpse of the sea beyond balsamy fir woods and wild plums that hang in their filmy bloom. So imagine a commercial for Hidden Valley ranch salad dressing.

With vintage elements that add to its rustic charm, the house is perfectly suited to the daily rhythms and hobbies of this "modern family." Matthew spends long days in the barn, milking the cows, baling hay, and writing a blog about how to adapt his farming practices to Brooklyn rooftops. If women come to the house, he hides in a small room off the parlor. When she is not in the depths of despair, Anne enjoys reading poetry about fairies, being rageful about Gilbert Blythe, and gallivanting about the forest with her bosom friend, Diana, who is dull but sweet and pretty.

It is a warm, if regimented, home, and Marilla is in charge. Because she is very into cleanliness, she scrubs the floor five times a day. When she is not doing this, she makes thousands of baking-powder biscuits, updates her recipe cards, and occasionally has a tipple of currant wine (the minister said it's fine). Sometimes Anne does the dishes, if she's not pretending to be a dead woman floating in a stream. Matthew doesn't do any housework because he is a man, which also means that he has a meal of jellied chicken and cold tongue served promptly when he returns from the fields.

"We try to keep things at Green Gables very farm-to-table," Marilla ejaculates. "Sustainability is everything around here, especially in the long winters, because without it, you will literally die."

Marilla was kind enough to sit down with us over crab-apple preserves and tea to discourse about the Cuthberts' decorating journey, although she did say that she was missing her Aid Society meeting.

She used the special dishes.

A CHAT WITH MARILLA

HER STYLE

My style is minimalist, and it doesn't matter what Matthew's style is because he has no say. I like bare country churches, clean lines, and furniture that embodies self-denial. My favorite chair is duly plain, but it's perfect for shelling peas or reading Revelation. My taste runs to quilts that contain no more than three colors and samplers embroidered with religious wisdom. I always say: You can never have too many samplers with the Word of Our Lord on them—anything that says to your guests, *We are not heathens, we swear.* Gosh, I wonder if they make a sampler with that on it.

IMPORTANT INFLUENCES

Well, first and foremost, I would say God. I see Our Lord as the original Property Brother, but of course there's only one of him, and he doesn't live in Las Vegas. And then Anne has been a big influence, although she likes to imagine her room as a kind of organdy-and-silk palace. She's very into imagining things, like that she has an alabaster brow and nut-brown hair, or that she's a princess or the Lady of the Lake. She carries around this book by Alfred, Lord Tennismatch or something like that.

FAVORITE ELEMENT

For me, definitely my kitchen, but Matthew's favorite design element is the barn, which is decorated with old rusty nails and bats. Once, someone told him he should hang up these big signs that read JOY and FAMILY, and he just looked at him like he was insane. I also like our front porch. Sometimes Rachel will come over to sit in the out-of-doors with me and speculate wildly about where people are headed in their buggies. She likes to make sure that respectable young ladies do not go driving with men. *Sluts,* she always says. But she prides herself on speaking her mind.

POTENTIAL IMPROVEMENTS

Anne wishes that we had another spare room. She's totally obsessed with spare rooms. I don't get it—I mean, we have one. She also likes to rename rooms in the house, so the porch is now the Veranda of Vision, and the toilet is the Privy of the Blooming Bowels. And she'd like to get rid of her bed and sleep in a wild cherry tree, but she had an imaginary friend who lived in an enchanted bookcase when she was a kid, so you know: crazysauce. The only kind of bookcase I will tolerate is a simple, economical model from a reliable supplier like West Elm.

WHAT FRIENDS SAY

Sometimes Rachel will tell me how she would have done something differently, like how we shouldn't have put a desk in Anne's room because now she'll start reading books and thinking about things and not get married.

BIGGEST EMBARRASSMENT

The time that Anne served Diana currant wine and got the girl completely wasted. That was a pretty kettle of fish. And in my parlor. Diana is a lush.

PROUDEST DIY

Setting up Anne's room. When I thought we were getting a boy, I figured he could sleep on the couch in the kitchen chamber, but that didn't seem right for a girl, even if she was a redheaded stray waif. So I set her up in the east gable room, which was decorated with bare whitewashed walls, plain window sashes, and a braided mat in the middle of the bare floor. She said that the room had a rigidity not to be described in words that sent a chill to the very marrow of her bones, but she would do the place up like Liberace if I left it to her. A less-is-more approach is better—nothing featherbrained. Just last week, I was reading in *Real Simple* that I should throw away everything I own and then buy other things that the magazine

helpfully suggests, and I was like, But I only own a pincushion and an amethyst brooch bequeathed to my mother by a seafaring uncle.

BIGGEST INDULGENCE

I sprang for a Viking range and marble countertops in the kitchen, but I passed on the seafoam-green Smeg fridge as it was too small to hold all my jars of jam. I see these purchases as adding value to Green Gables in the long run—everyone on *House Hunters* wants a chef's kitchen, even though none of those deadbeats can even make a grilled cheese. We also put in some stylish open shelving to store my muffins, raspberry cordial, and medicine for grippe.

BIGGEST CHALLENGE

Trying to bleach the muslin curtains for the third time in a week while Anne is going on and on about how she wishes that roses could talk because they would say such lovely things. And making the house "green." If you have a farmhouse, it has to be green. We put in structural insulated panels, an insulated concrete form foundation, and blown-in cellulose insulation in the attic. Overall, we tried to use materials that were locally sourced or salvaged. But listen to me! Boy, do I sound smug. God would not like that.

BEST ADVICE

Only listen to the decorating advice of kindred spirits because everyone, and I mean everyone, is fixing up old farmhouses these days. Really, the thing is not to be afraid to sit down with a notebook full of Sears catalogue cutouts and mix elements that don't necessarily go together, like a painting of "Christ Blessing the Little Children" and a Barcelona chair. But don't go overboard. You can always enliven a room with a throw pillow covered in burlap or a single flower in a vase. And as Anne says, without the right paint scheme for a historic home, your life will be a perfect graveyard of buried hopes.

DECORATING CHALLENGES: RICHES TO RAGS WITH LITTLE PRINCESS SARA CREWE

"When my father, Captain Crewe, sort of but not really died, I found that I had to think about decorating my new attic space at Miss Minchin's Select Seminary for Young Ladies on a budget. This was a shock to me: I had always had everything I wanted, from sable and ermine on my coats to Valenciennes lace on my underclothing. My dad really likes to shop. He would buy me all sorts of things and then go back to India to do his good work there. If you can come by some soft ostrich feathers left over from the good old days of your extreme wealth, I suggest displaying them in your dark attic room. Their beauty will distract you from the sound of mice and make you feel like less of a drudge."

Maria von Trapp, The Story of the Trapp Family Singers

MARIA AND GEORG'S ANTI-FASCIST, MUSIC-FILLED SALZBURG LAKE HOUSE

Names: Maria, former-postulant-turned-wife who now dons fabulous tweed suits, and Captain Georg von Trapp, retired officer of the Imperial Navy and handsome devil

Location: Salzburg, Austria

Size: A large house with very extensive grounds, and Georg *will not have anyone shouting*

Years lived in together: For some time whilst Maria was the plucky governess, and now as a married couple; owned

RECENTLY RETURNED from their honeymoon where they finally got to have a lot of sex, Maria and Georg have already set to work on making improvements to their lovely lakefront mountain home. Maria, who has made a career change, is surprised to find herself in charge of such a large house.

"I was going to be a nun, but Georg was a tall drink of espresso," she says. "With one of those little chocolates on the side."

Their historic house has a number of exquisite period features, including Louis XV gold paneling and sufficient crystal chandeliers to outfit an ice palace, but the couple has also made some modern updates.

"The patio off the ballroom was all fine and good for dancing the Ländler and blushing uncontrollably in Georg's arms," says Maria. "But it was time to rethink those tall hedges and fake Greek statues. We got a fire pit, some new patio furniture, and a copper Weber for grilling in the summer. We really hit up Lowe's."

Georg hadn't done a lot to the house since the death of his saintly wife, who no doubt kicked the bucket because she had popped out seven children. But Maria has proven the perfect governess, decorator, and now mother, even with her short hair.

"Salzburg is spectacular," she says. "The city is known for its delightful berry picking, twittering birds, green hills, great climbing trees, and impending Anschluss. I'm a big fan of the hills."

Her former home of the abbey has also been a decorating inspiration.

"I have tried to incorporate some design elements from the world I abandoned to take my proper place in the patriarchy," she says. "I found the loveliest white Italian leather couch from Ruggiero e Hammerstein that looks like a huge wimple."

She has also ordered a number of things that will arrive in brown paper packages tied up with string.

While Maria enjoys spending her afternoons reupholstering furniture in old curtain fabric, the transition to domestic, married life has been a challenge for Georg, who is preoccupied not only with what kind of countertop will prove most durable in their kitchen but also with the rise of fascism.

"Georg has been gardening to deal with his stress," Maria says. "Mostly, he plants a lot of Edelweiss and takes swigs out of his flask and cries."

A CHAT WITH MARIA

THEIR STYLE

Georg favors a seafaring aesthetic inspired by rigid discipline, uniforms, and a lot of marching. He likes rooms to conduct themselves with the utmost order and decorum. I enjoy large fountains, tree-lined streets,

extravagant home puppet theaters, and statues that remind me of the Reverend Mother's chiseled cheekbones.

IMPORTANT INFLUENCES

For Georg, definitely nature. We were repainting the children's rooms, and he wanted something that suggested "the wind that moves through the trees like a restless sea," and I was like, Georg, seriously—that's not a color.

INSPIRATION

Uncle Max has a great eye. He and Rolfe used to go furniture shopping from time to time before Rolfe dropped off the face of the earth. They picked out a gorgeous Saarinen Womb Chair and an Ümlaut side chair upholstered in the color "Auf Wiedersehen."

SOME OF HER FAVORITE THINGS

Oh, my lord—I have more favorite things than Oprah. I love my Switzerland Sofa from Mitchell Gold + Bob Williams, which I picked up during their 20% Off Living Room Event, as well as my Bright Copper Kettle armchair from Victor + Victoria. And I'm obsessed with my retro powder-blue AGA Dual Control cooker, which I suppose isn't really retro as the fifties haven't happened yet. I cook all the time. Whenever I make schnitzel with noodles, Georg says, Sweetie, you need to Instagram that shit.

BIGGEST INDULGENCE

Our housekeeper, Frau Schmidt. I really couldn't do without her stern and haughty glare—and her help around the house. She has very high standards for herself and others. I mean, it's 1938, and the woman dresses like a character in an Oscar Wilde play.

CHANGES TO THE PROPERTY

Liesl had us tear down the gazebo because she has bad memories of Rolfe telling her that he was seventeen going on eighteen and would take care of her, and then, you know, he became a Nazi.

INTERMISSION AND ENTR'ACTE

WHAT FRIENDS SAY

Georg's friends from his days in Vienna's glittering salons seem to like the place, and they stop by for sachertorte and to remind us how much better it is to live in the city. The Baroness says our wine cellar is lacking and that I could up my fashion game. Max drops in for pink lemonade laced with pink lemonade and to blather on about his career woes. I don't really have any friends since I left the sisterhood. All my nun friends stood behind a big, dramatic gate at my wedding, and I thought, You seriously have to stand behind that gate? You can't even come in and hang out with me? Jesus.

BIGGEST EMBARRASSMENT

Those Nazi bastards hung their spider flag in front of the house, and it has zero curb appeal.

UPGRADES TO THE PROPERTY

We just put in a spa bathroom with Jack and Jill sinks, and now our mornings go so much more smoothly. I don't understand how couples manage with just one sink. Imagine that! At the abbey, I would just wash with a bowl of icy, not quite clean water, but you won't find me doing that self-abnegating nonsense anymore.

PLANS FOR THE FUTURE

We're actually considering a move, perhaps into the mountains, on foot in the middle of the night. Otherwise, Georg will be forced to relocate to a submarine of the Third Reich, and those spaces are absurdly cramped—much smaller and less cool than tiny houses.

BEST ADVICE

Don't rely too heavily on trends, and follow your own heart. And don't be intimidated by problems. How do you solve a problem like a lack of throw pillows? Just go to Target and get some more friggin' throw pillows.

DECORATING WITH HEIDI

"I was left with my grandfather, who lives all alone in the mountains of Dörfli. He never talked to anyone in the village and hadn't set foot in church for years. Real recluse. I wanted our cottage to be a more inviting and organized space—like a cute little music box. My taste is inspired by a mock-Bavarian tourist village I saw in America. It was adorable. Way better than real Bavaria. I took a couple of Grandfather's colorful ceramic beer steins and filled them with wild flowers. I styled the coffee table with a pair of decorative wooden shoes and a folk-art dish depicting sheep. And finally, I hung up some cuckoo clocks. About ten, I believe. It's a little scary when they go off all at once, but hey, birds are scary."

INTERLUDE:
CHOOSING ART FOR YOUR HOME

For some, the art in your home should demonstrate your taste and sophistication. For others, it should match the sofa. From frame clusters to large signature pieces, the options can seem limitless—and intimidating. Dorian Gray and the Duke in Robert Browning's "My Last Duchess" offer tips for what to do with all that wall space.

DUKE: So let me show you around my place. I have a magnificent collection of art. That's my last Duchess painted on the wall.

DORIAN: She looks as if she were alive.

DUKE: It's a wonder. You simply cannot do better than Fra Pandolf for portraits of duchesses.

DORIAN: Never heard of him.

DUKE: Seriously? He's famous, you philistine. Now you're going to tell me that you don't know Claus of Innsbruck.

DORIAN: I . . .

DUKE: Unreal. Anyway. You want to look for the depth and passion of an earnest glance in a painting. If you are distinguished like myself and have a nine-hundred-year-old name.

DORIAN: That is a really old name.

DUKE: Thanks. It is.

DORIAN: I think you can never go wrong with a portrait. Why do people want all these bland landscapes in their homes? But that is the English for you. You Italians are rather more emotional than we are.

DUKE: Emotional. Yes.

DORIAN: So I have a portrait of myself. When I first saw it, I thought that it was beautiful because I am beautiful. Have you noticed how beautiful I am? You haven't said anything about it, as other people tend to do.

DUKE: You are indeed a good-looking man.

DORIAN: I am a fucking vision. But I am jealous of everything whose beauty does not die. I was jealous of the portrait painted of me. It seemed to me that every moment that passed took something from me and gave something to it.

DUKE: I suppose we all see different things when we look at art. My last Duchess, she had a heart—how shall I say?—too soon made glad, too easily impressed; she liked whate'er she looked on, and her looks went everywhere.

DORIAN: Bit of a . . .

DUKE: Some would say "tart," but not me! Although officious fools were always breaking boughs of cherries for her in the orchard.

DORIAN: There is absolutely nothing worse than an officious fool bearing cherries.

DUKE: I quite agree. See that expression in the painting? She's smiling. I mean, I know there are other paintings of smiling, or not smiling, women out there. But this one is really extraordinary.

DORIAN: She had a lovely smile.

DUKE: She did. Although she did kind of smile at everyone. Men, I mean. Not that I minded! Why would I mind? I'm just saying.

DORIAN: Right.

DUKE: I gave commands; then all smiles stopped together.

DORIAN: That's really none of my . . .

DUKE: But now I keep her behind a curtain so she only smiles for me.

DORIAN: Nice. I came across a large, purple satin coverlet heavily embroidered with gold and thought it would serve to wrap my portrait in—it became rather dreadful, this portrait. I wanted to hide something that had a corruption of its own, worse than the corruption of death itself—something that would breed horrors and yet would never die.

DUKE: Coverlets are quite good for that.

DORIAN: So where is your Duchess now?

DUKE: Oh, she, um . . . she died.

DORIAN: Oh.

DUKE: Yep.

DORIAN: I'm sorry.

DUKE: It was because of the smiling.

DORIAN: Gosh, is that the time? You know, it was so nice of you to have me over, but I should be heading home.

DUKE: I also have a bronze seahorse.

V.

QUIRKY DWELLINGS

Herman Melville, Moby Dick

ISHMAEL'S WHITE-WHALE-WORTHY SHIP OF DREAMS

Name: Call him Ishmael

Location: In the unshored, harborless immensities of the sea

Size: Rather small, if anything

Years lived in: For some time—never mind how long precisely; worked on (not owned or rented)

SOMETIMES THERE IS NOTHING like a change of scene. One day, having little or no money in his purse, and nothing particular to interest him on shore, Ishmael thought he would sail about a little and see the watery part of the world. He describes his time at sea as a way of driving off the spleen and regulating the circulation, as well as a "good alternative to jumping in front of oncoming traffic or throwing myself on my sword, Cato-style."

He found his dream ship in the form of the fated *Pequod*, a vessel known for her voyages in search of portentous and mysterious monsters of the deep. The *Pequod* is no quaint craft—not like those square-toed luggers, mountainous Japanese junks, butter-box galliots, and whatnot. She is a rare old craft, a ship of the old school with an old-fashioned claw-footed look about her. Long seasoned and weather-stained in the typhoons and calms of all four oceans, her old hull's complexion is darkened like a French grenadier's, who has alike fought in Egypt and Siberia, or a spray-tanned Hollywood starlet at an awards show.

"Her masts—cut somewhere on the coast of Japan, where her original ones were lost overboard in a gale—her masts stand stiffly up like the spines of the three old kings of Cologne," says Ishmael. "Her ancient decks are worn and wrinkled, like the pilgrim-worshipped flagstone in Canterbury Cathedral where Becket bled. I know I'm kind of overdoing it with the similes, but it's hard to describe her. She is ideally suited to encounter all the terrors of the pitiless maw of the lone Atlantic, and the deck is an excellent space for pacing about in a maniacal manner."

The ship's Captain Ahab is fond of this activity, as he is of gazing. While pertinaciously pursuing one particular whale that dismembered him in an almost fatal encounter, Ahab enjoys privacy and polar bear pelts. When not toiling by lantern, some of the crew can be found lounging opposite the mouth of the tryworks, where the windlass serves for a sea sofa.

"I wish that the scuttle were larger," he says. "But my heart will go on."

With her whalebone den and venerable, vindictive bows thrust into the cold malicious waves, the *Pequod* offers mobile living for those who feel their feet are scorched by the land. From bow to stern, living is communal, and space is at a premium. And although Ishmael sometimes finds life on a ship "a little claustrophobic," he is drawn like the magnetic needle of a compass to the *Pequod*'s nautical details and her all-American wood, worthy of a hearse.

"Anchors really ground a space," he says. "You have your harpoons, your binnacle lamps, your ropes, your muskets, your hammocks. I have a friend who thinks that embalmed New Zealand heads make lovely curios, and I'm inclined to agree with him. Apart from the heads of dead idolaters, you can do worse than a picture of Jonah or Job. And an old-fashioned oaken chair, wriggling all over with curious carvings, will always pair well with ropes and old sails. Or new sails, if you decide to treat yourself!"

A CHAT WITH ISHMAEL

HIS STYLE

Nantucket meets Quaker, with a dash of Cape Cod and Satan. And cozy, I would say. The ship's sleeping quarters are the definition of cozy, and the grand, ungodly, godlike Captain Ahab refers to them as "thy nightly grave," so that's nice. We all like candles. Honestly, it requires a strong moral principle to prevent me from buying every candle I see that looks like it is moving about in a tomb! Lovely effect. And there is a ruggedness to the ship's aesthetic. It has aged well from the rain, spray, sun, and wind of the robust and manlike sea. We get the occasional rot, which also adds a feeling of authenticity. People pay a fortune to make things look old, but all we have to do is go to sea for years and years.

IMPORTANT INFLUENCES

Whales, certainly—of your Jonathan Adler variety or something more traditional. Ivory is always a strong choice, whether for a set of knives or a peg leg. Or bone, of course. The *Pequod* is a cannibal of a craft, tricking herself forth in the chased bones of her enemies. I'm also inspired by the style of inns with names like "The Crossed Harpoons" and "The Spouter-Inn." I'm really into harpoons and things that spout.

FAVORITE ELEMENT

I like to blend old and new. To the *Pequod*'s old antiquities, we added new and marvelous features pertaining to the wild business that for more than half a century she has followed. Old Captain Peleg built upon her original grotesqueness, and inlaid it, all over, with a quaintness both of material and device, unmatched by anything except it be Thorkill-Hake's carved buckler or bedstead. I imagine you're familiar with that work.

WHAT FRIENDS SAY

I know that almost all men in their degree, some time or other, have cherished very nearly the same feelings towards the *Pequod* as I do. My friend Jack Aubrey admires the lovely views of the sky from the quarterdeck. And we ran into a chap named Wentworth some time ago, and he admired her unpanelled, open bulwarks, which are garnished like one continuous jaw, with the long sharp teeth of the sperm whale inserted in there for pins. He also talked an awful lot about this woman Anne he had left back home. Poor sap.

BIGGEST CHALLENGE

Finding a place for everything. Whaling ships are known for their maximalist aesthetic as you need three years' worth of housekeeping when you're far from all grocers, costermongers, doctors, bakers, and bankers. And whaling vessels are exposed to accidents of all kinds, especially to the destruction and loss of the very things upon which the success of the voyage depends. I mean, how unfair is that? So from beef, bread, water, fuel, iron hoops and staves, bolts of canvas, and coils of rigging to long oil-ladles and still longer whaling lances, everything must be both attractive and useful for pursuing a murderous monster continually athirst for human blood.

BIGGEST EMBARRASSMENT

Sometimes you do miss the comforts of land, although truth be told, land isn't very comfortable either. In the inn where I stayed before setting off, there was a rude shelf, a papered fireboard representing man striking a whale, a crazy old sea chest and a prodigious bed, almost big enough for four harpooners to sleep abreast. It may well have been stuffed with corn-cobs or crockery, and I had to sleep with Queequeg, who smoked in bed and had a tomahawk pipe and a Congo idol—and as we slept, he threw his arm over me like I was his wife, and I didn't really know what to do about that—but I always say: Better to sleep with a sober cannibal than a drunk Christian. I really do always say that. I have had occasion to say it more than once.

BIGGEST INDULGENCE

Captain Ahab's quarters are quite exclusive. He talks about the "masoned, walled town of a Captain's exclusiveness," which the guys and I think has something to do with solitude and loneliness. At any rate, he likes to keep to himself. Sometimes he stands in his pivot hole or in the scuttle for a whole hour on the stretch, and the unheeded night damp gathers in beads of dew upon his stone-carved coat and hat. He does a lot of standing.

PROUDEST DIY

Mending old sails.

BEST ADVICE

Should I share the secrets of the currents of the sea that have never yet been divulged? Just kidding! I will. Regarding materials, remember how immaterial are all materials! What things are there, but imponderable thoughts? And—if you're lucky—some broiled fowl, judiciously buttered.

DECORATING CHALLENGES WITH RALPH OF *LORD OF THE FLIES*

"Maybe we should have thought more about a shelter after the crash. Something civilized, like the dorm rooms back at our English boarding school that trapped us in a cycle of violence and cruelty that haunts us still. Instead, we just ended up with a lot of fires and a dumb conch."

PIPPI'S UNREGULATED AND POTENTIALLY DANGEROUS VILLA OF PANDEMONIUM

Name: Pippi Longstocking (full name Pippilotta Delicatessa Windowshade Mackrelmint Efraim's Daughter Longstocking), a strong and remarkable child with hair the color of a carrot styled in two tight braids that stick straight out, a nose the shape of a very small potato, and freckles

Location: Sweden, way out at the end of a tiny little town, where the street turns into a country road

Size: Plenty of room for her

Years lived in: Nine years (but purchased by her father long ago); owned

You have only to look for the overgrown garden at the edge of town to find nine-year-old Pippi Longstocking's old house, where she lives alone because she does not have a mother or a father. While the loss of both of one's parents might be regarded as a misfortune—or even look like carelessness—Pippi loves the independence that comes with solitary living. There is no one to tell her to go to bed just when she is having the most fun, and no one to make her take cod-liver oil when she much prefers caramel candy.

"My mother died when I was just a tiny baby in my cradle, and my father was a sea captain who sailed on the great ocean, and sometimes I sailed with him, until one day he was blown overboard in a storm and disappeared," she says. "It was annoying."

She likes to think that her mother is in heaven, watching over her through a peephole in the sky, and that her father, Captain Efraim Longstocking, survived the storm and was washed ashore on an island of cannibals and became their cannibal king. No remotely sensible child psychologist would let this kind of thinking go unchecked, but Pippi does not have a child psychologist.

But she does have a funky and eclectic house, Villa Villekulla, to which she returned after the storm washed her father away. In the garden is a tumbledown gate and a gravel path bordered with old moss-covered trees. A pear tree grows close to the fence and stretches its branches low so that children can sit and pick the best little red-gold pears, which comes in handy as Pippi doesn't have anyone to feed her. There is also an old hollow tree where she stashes things like leather notebooks and red coral necklaces that represent a tenuous connection to the social world from which she is almost entirely alienated. She also hosts coffee parties in this tree and throws the cups down on the grass to "see how strong the china they make these days is."

Villa Villekulla is much roomier than her father's ship, where she lived for some time as they traveled the world. When she arrived at the house, she brought no more than a monkey named Mr. Nilsson, whom she dresses in a little suit because animals love wearing clothes, and a big suitcase full of gold pieces.

The villa is complemented by her sartorial style. Her dress, which she made herself, is rather unusual. She meant it to be blue, but there wasn't quite enough blue cloth, so she sewed little red pieces on here and there, and on her long, thin legs, she wears a pair of long stockings, one brown and the other black.

"I also have a pair of black shoes that are twice as long as my feet, which my father bought for me in South America so I would have something to grow into," she says. "South America is one of the places I have been lucky enough to see. It's quite savage, which is how my dad taught me to talk about places that are not Sweden."

Pippi fancies herself quite the open-minded and knowledgeable world traveler.

"I once saw a Chinese in Shanghai," she adds. "His ears were so big that he could use them for a cape. When it rained he just crawled in under his ears and was as warm and snug as you please. You find out so much about other cultures when you travel. Like how you're superior to them because you're from Sweden."

The house has a shingled roof that Pippi can climb out on to escape any form of adult authority. And if necessary, she is able to draw on her never-really-explained superhuman strength to remove meddling police officers from her property. Indeed, she occasionally gets angry but says that this is "not at all about losing my mother when I was an infant."

Pippi enjoys rhubarb pudding, morning promenades, picnics of ham and meatball sandwiches, ghosts, circuses where you can see giants on display, tramps who dance the schottische, and bulls that appear out of nowhere. She does not enjoy things that are tiresome or exasperating. She also loves to tell utterly absorbing stories to her next-door neighbors Tommy and Annika, who are very well-behaved and do have parents.

Her favorite room is the kitchen, where she makes eggs with shells in them.

"In Brazil, all the people go about with eggs in their hair, and there are no bald-headed people. That's the kind of valuable cultural insight you learn from traveling with a great dad like mine."

A CHAT WITH PIPPI

HER STYLE

Unconventional, but also neat. Sometimes I forget to do my Friday cleaning, but I like to keep the place generally tidy. I clean the kitchen floor by strapping scrubbing brushes to my bare feet, which is kind of like going ice-skating at the holidays, although I never get to do that because I'm so totally alone. But I'm happy to make a royal mess at someone else's house. Once I went to a party at the Settergrens' next door. They had a wonderful coffee table, and their fire was burning brightly, and they had a sofa and a photo album, and the ladies talked about their problems with their servants. Then Ella the maid brought out all these cakes, and I heaped as many as I could onto my plate, threw five lumps of sugar into a coffee cup, and placed the plate of cakes between my toes and dunked the cakes in my coffee and stuffed so many in my mouth that I couldn't have uttered a word no matter how hard I tried. Mrs. Settergren said that she was going to write to Philip Galanes about it.

IMPORTANT INFLUENCES

I'd love to bring in some details from Farthest India and Egypt, but I don't know if I could find exotic accessories like that here in my little Swedish town. I had a fight with a dreadful snake in India once. He ate five Indians and then two little children for dessert every day. When we went to Egypt, I learned that people walk backward there—you know, like in the paintings. Isn't that funny? My dad taught me that people who aren't Swedish aren't really people. He was such a wonderful dad.

FAVORITE ELEMENT

My horse. He is my best friend. I can even lift him if I want to, because I'm so strong. I bought him with one of the many gold pieces in my suitcase, and he lives on the porch because he would be in the way in the kitchen, and he doesn't like the parlor. If I want to drink my afternoon coffee there, as kids do, I just lift him and set him down in the garden. I also love my bed: I always sleep with my feet on the pillow and my head way down under the quilt, the way they do in Guatemala. It's because I know things like that thing about Guatemala that I don't have to go to school. Oh, and in Argentina, it's against the law to have lessons.

KEY FEATURE

My huge chest in the parlor. It's the only piece of furniture in there. I mean, who needs couches and chairs when you have the total freedom of an abandoned child? In the chest are many tiny drawers containing all my treasures, such as birds' eggs, strange shells and stones, pretty little boxes, lovely silver mirrors, pearl necklaces, and many other things that my dad and I bought on our journeys around the world because we have money. Once, when I was in the jungles of Borneo, I found a wooden leg! Imagine that, right in the heart of the forest! In a place that no human being had ever set foot before. You know, now that I think of it, maybe someone had been there, or else how would the wooden leg have gotten there?

WHAT FRIENDS SAY

All the ladies and gentlemen in town found out that I was living alone here and thought that I should be put in a children's home, but I said that I already had a place in a children's home because I was a child and this was my home. You see what I did there? That's the kind of thinking on your feet that you need while you're waiting for your cannibal-king dad to return and claim you.

BIGGEST EMBARRASSMENT

Not my white privilege! I don't even know what that means because I'm nine, and my dad never taught me.

PROUDEST DIY

I painted a large picture on the wallpaper in the parlor. The picture represents a fat lady in a red dress and a black hat. In one hand she holds a yellow flower, and in the other, a dead rat. So you can see I'm doing just fine.

BIGGEST INDULGENCE

I don't always tell the truth, but I like to see that as one of my kooky and charming characteristics and not as a deeply troubling form of escapism. You know, there is not a single person in the Congo who tells the truth. They lie all day long. Begin at seven in the morning and keep on until sundown. God, I'm just filled with fun facts about foreign cultures.

PLANS FOR THE FUTURE

When my dad comes back, we're going to go back to his cannibal island, and I will be a cannibal princess. He says that the cannibals want us to be their rulers. What a dad.

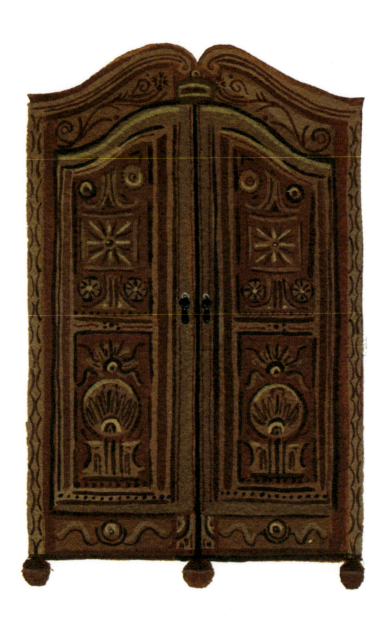

C. S. Lewis, The Lion, the Witch and the Wardrobe

THE PROFESSOR'S BOOK-FILLED BACHELOR PAD FOR CHILDREN FLEEING AIR RAIDS

Name: The Professor, who is a professor

Location: In the heart of the English countryside, ten miles from the nearest railway station and two miles from the nearest post office

Size: Very large (far larger than any house Lucy had ever been in before)

Years lived in: Probably a while as the Professor is an old man with shaggy white hair that grows over most of his face as well as on his head; owned

THE REPUTATION of the Professor's house is legendary. In fact, the house is so old and famous that people from all over England come and ask permission to see it. It is the sort of house that is mentioned in guidebooks and even in histories, and it might as well be, for all manner of stories are told about it. The perfectly splendid property boasts a wireless, a lot of books, an odd-looking front door, a balcony, long passages and rows of doors leading into empty rooms, a Green Room, and the relentless sound of owls.

The Professor has no wife (just never met the right woman) and lives with his housekeeper, Mrs. Macready, and three servants, whose names are Ivy, Margaret, and Betty, but they do not matter. He works at an unnamed university and looks like a professor because he is a man and white and old.

He describes himself as an "introvert," but he doesn't stay cooped up in his wonderfully odd house all the time.

"I'm part of an informal club called the Inklings, which meets at the pub to discuss books," he says. "We have a lot of great ideas and are geniuses."

He is most at home in his library, breathing in centuries of mold from old books and reflecting on how long it will be possible to keep women out of the academy. When parties of sightseers arrive and ask to see the house, he always gives them permission.

"I'm fortunate to live in such a unique house, but I leave the tours to Mrs. Macready," he says, taking off his spectacles and beginning to polish them. "She shows them around, telling them about the pictures and the armor and the rare books in the library. Mrs. Macready is not fond of children, which is strange as she's a woman. But she really gets the dust off all my editions of Shakespeare."

Mrs. Macready has recently found herself with four children underfoot, but she was sure to tell them to keep out of the way when she was taking a party through the house. Peter, Susan, Edmund, and Lucy were rescued from the air raids in London, which are both a plot device and a real bummer of a thing in history.

They appreciate their new home as it is filled with unexpected places, and you never seem to come to the end of it. They often play hide-and-seek while the Professor rearranges pieces of paper and clears his throat.

A CHAT WITH THE PROFESSOR

HIS STYLE

Complicated. Even a bit confusing. I like an aesthetic that doesn't reveal itself right away. Lucy calls it "a little creepy," but the kids like it—it's the sort of house where no one minds what they do. In fact, no one can hear one another as it's about ten minutes' walk from the bedrooms down to the dining room, with any amount of stairs and passages in between. Can you walk for ten minutes in your house? I didn't think so.

HIS INSPIRATION

I should warn you that this is a very strange house, and even I know very little about it. But Oxford is an inspiration, if not Oxford commas. The city has some buildings that are almost as nice as my house. And so much of my inspiration comes from my books. There is a whole series of rooms that lead into each other and are lined with books—most of them very old books and some bigger than the Bible in a church. I think I have more books than Karl Lagerfeld. Nice try, Lagerfeld.

INTERESTING FEATURES

The house has an incredible location. We have lots of mountains and animals in those mountains. Stags, eagles, hawks, foxes, rabbits, and badgers—you name it. And a garden with a stream. It's a pleasant place to walk around and read the complete works of Milton aloud to yourself.

IMPORTANT PIECES

I have a lot of armor, which might be surprising as I'm a non-violent liberal professor type. But there is a long room full of pictures and a suit of armor, and a room all hung with green, with a harp in one corner. Peter says that you might find anything in a place like this. But that makes sense as I'm a very remarkable man.

BIGGEST SPLURGE

My desk set. My fountain pen is my life.

MOST MAGICAL FEATURE

The wardrobe is a very alarming subject, but yes: the wardrobe. It isn't your average mothball-smelling wardrobe as it serves as a portal into another world, where there are things like Turkish delight and sleds and big, sad lions who sacrifice themselves for you, which reminds me of someone else who did that, but I'm forgetting who at this particular moment.

The wardrobe has a looking glass in the door and is located in a room that is quite empty otherwise. That's the sort of quirky thing we professor types do: decorate a room with only a wardrobe! But the room is also accented with a dead bluebottle on the windowsill, for a little something extra. The wardrobe is filled with fur coats with pockets full of camphor. I know, I know: fur coats. I get it. Fur is bad. I don't wear them.

WHAT FRIENDS SAY

My students seem to like it. I have the occasional pupil over to tell him that his knowledge of Cicero is pathetic. One day, I asked Edmund if he was named after Edmund in *King Lear*, and he said, "What is *King Lear*?" Bless me, what *do* they teach the kids at these schools? They probably don't even know Latin and Greek.

PROUDEST DIY

Setting up the kids' room. I set apart a long, low room for them with two windows looking out in one direction and two in another. I have heard that kids like windows. And puppies. But I don't have any of those.

BIGGEST CHALLENGE

Making room for the children. That was tough, but I find that I like their company in spite of their insufficient educations. They say things like, "If things are real, they're there all the time," and I say, "Are they?" to mess with them, which is fun to do to displaced children in times of major political crises. Their preoccupation with hiding and escaping into other worlds may have something to do with the war, but it's also adorable.

PLANS FOR THE FUTURE

Lucy has been asking if we can get a stone table, preferably one cut all over with strange lines and figures that might be the letters of an unknown language. I keep telling her it's not the sort of thing we're going to find in town. For my part, I plan to keep doing my professor things, like smoking and sitting in chairs. I'd also like to put some statues in the courtyard—but real statues, not creatures that have been frozen into statues by an evil, majestic-lion-killing, one-might-say-frigid-but-I-didn't White Witch. Yes. This place *could* use a woman's touch, but I just never met the right woman.

BEST ADVICE

Read the classics.

HOW TO SET UP A CHILD-FRIENDLY HOME AWAY FROM HOME WITH MEDEA

"As an exile, I have been wondering: Do you adopt your new home wholeheartedly or try to bring in elements of your past? And couples sometimes have different styles, which is certainly the case with Jason and me. I'd like to merge his Corinthian style with my barbarian one. I'm hoping to discuss this with him, but he's never around anymore. God, the things I have done for that man. For now, I'm focusing on the kids. I ordered some new bedroom furniture for them from the Land of Nod. And I'm really enjoying the palace's open-plan kitchen, which allows me to watch them while they play. I sure have been watching them a lot lately."

Charles Perkins Gilman, "The Yellow Wallpaper"

UNNAMED NEURASTHENIC NARRATOR'S
YELLOW-WALLPAPERED REST AND RECOVERY ROOM

Names: Unnamed Neurasthenic Narrator, who is kept in a room (where she takes phosphates or phosphites—whichever it is—and tonics), and her husband, John, a physician of high standing and practitioner of pseudoscience

Location: Somewhere you definitely do not want to be, three miles from the village

Size: Unnamed Neurasthenic Narrator doesn't really know as her movements are limited

Years lived in: For the summer; rented

I T IS VERY SELDOM that mere ordinary people secure ancestral halls for the summer. But then, sometimes they do. A hereditary estate! The absolute height of romantic felicity.

Unnamed Neurasthenic Narrator (possibly "Jane"?) was initially suspicious of the cheapness of the rent for her summer home, as well as the fact that the house had stood so long untenanted, but her practical-in-the-extreme husband, John, simply laughed at her because women and their notions are hilarious. Unnamed Neurasthenic Narrator believed that congenial work, with excitement and change, would do her good, but John insisted that being an invalid is really the best thing for women. And this colonial mansion was just the place.

"We snapped it up," she says. "I was so excited to have a place to write, although writing does exhaust me a great deal. Due to my temporary nervous depression—a slight hysterical tendency—I am absolutely forbidden to 'work' until I am well again. This includes writing. And reflecting on how the Gilded Age of the 1880s challenged a number of conventional ideas about women's (decorating) roles, even as it also affirmed many traditional understandings of gender identity."

The house is known for its nursery, where Unnamed Neurasthenic Narrator is confined on account of her nervous condition. The room is wallpapered in the color yellow and decorated with mismatched, inharmonious furniture brought from downstairs. The floor is scratched and gouged and splintered, and the plaster itself is dug out here and there. Since giving birth, Unnamed Neurasthenic Narrator spends every moment of her existence here, in a state of isolation that will no doubt make her feel much better in no time.

And she is more than a little preoccupied with the yellow wallpaper.

"At first John said he meant to repaper the room, but then he just left me here with it—and with my 'fancies,' as he calls them—and got on with his life, whatever that might involve. Not having babies, I can tell you that. The asshole doesn't have to do that."

But this cell-like confine for neurasthenic women is not the home's only intriguing feature. The house is a most beautiful place! It is quite alone, standing well back from the road. It brings to mind English places that you read about, for there are hedges and walls and gates that lock, and lots of separate little houses for the gardeners and people who are free and not locked up.

"There is a *delicious* garden. I never saw such a garden: large and shady, full of box-bordered paths, and lined with long grape-covered arbors with seats under them. And outside everything is green instead of yellow. Not that I really get to hang out in the garden, on account of this nervous lady condition that maybe one day the misogynist pricks—I mean, the medical establishment—will stop saying is a thing."

A CHAT WITH UNNAMED NEURASTHENIC NARRATOR

HER STYLE

I used to have a big, old bureau and a chair that always seemed like a strong friend. But not anymore. Now my style really comes down to this yellow wallpaper. It is pretty much my world. Some people just do a wall-papered accent wall, the kind you used to see all the time in *Domino*, but that's not for me. John laughs at me so about the wallpaper! I am pretty obsessed with it. It makes me think of all the yellow things I ever saw—not beautiful things like buttercups, but old, foul, bad yellow things. You might say that the wallpaper flawlessly fuses color and texture. The color is so hideous, and unreliable, and infuriating, and the pattern is even worse—really torturing. Like not having any purposeful or intellectual connection to the public sphere.

HER INSPIRATION

The pathologizing of the female body and a profound masculine fear of female sexuality in the age of the New Woman. And yellow. I asked John if we could replace the yellow wallpaper and maybe order a sample of that Graham & Brown wallpaper printed with bookshelves—you know, the kind in all the hipster bars—but John said that I'm not to read books, let alone write them, and to stop with my false and foolish fancies. And then he patted me on the head and left to go to the beach.

IMPORTANT FEATURE

There is a great heavy bed that looks as if it has been through the wars. It's actually *nailed to the floor*—what an idea!—and provides an excellent van-tage point for following the pointless pattern on the wallpaper to some sort

of a conclusion. Beds are great things to force women into when they're "exhausted." It's a cure, I'm told: taking to one's bed. But I swear to god, I'm bored out of my mind. I would even read Knausgård at this point.

FAVORITE ELEMENT

Did I mention the yellow wallpaper? The paper looks to me as if it *knows* what a vicious influence it has! There is a recurrent spot where the pattern lolls like a broken neck and two bulbous eyes stare at me upside down. I get positively angry with the impertinence of it and the everlastingness. Up and down and sideways they crawl, and those absurd, unblinking eyeballs are everywhere. I never saw so much expression in an inanimate thing before, including that IKEA commercial with the lamp left out in the rain. I told John that I didn't think that bulbous, unblinking eyeball wallpaper was a very good design feature, but he just called me a blessed little goose.

WHAT FRIENDS SAY

Probably that I have failed to perform my wifely duties. I'd love to have some people over, but John says that he doesn't want stimulating people around me. He says that he would as soon put fireworks in my pillowcase! I asked him to please not do that.

BIGGEST EMBARRASSMENT

According to John and his medical buddies, probably not taking care of my baby as it has been made crystal clear to me that this is my only value as a human being. I'm fortunate that John's sister is so good with the baby. She's pious, industrious, and domestic. What a fucking saint.

PROUDEST DIY

I tore down the wallpaper. I thought I could see a strange, provoking, formless figure that seemed to skulk about behind that silly and conspicuous front design. Yes, it was a dim subpattern, and I was quite sure it was a woman who shook the front pattern. So I decided that I needed to help her, and I pulled and she shook, and before morning we had peeled off yards of the paper. It's nice to have some help with DIY projects. She was great.

BIGGEST CHALLENGE

Thinking. John doesn't like me to think. He says that it's dangerous for a temperament like mine.

BIGGEST INDULGENCE

John would say my nervous condition is an indulgence, and he's a "doctor," so I suppose he would know. I used to think that John was really obsessed with decorating—I thought he was always talking about rooms—but then I realized that he was saying "wombs." Which is really not the same thing at all.

BEST ADVICE

Take a gender studies class.

LOVING YOUR HOME WITH QUEEN DIDO

"My city of Carthage is the best city anyone could ever imagine, and the signature piece is no doubt the mural of the Trojan War in my extraordinary temple. Murals aren't just for kids' room or Italian restaurants anymore. They're an excellent alternative to wallpaper, gallery walls, and the oversized art trend. And you can really make them work in a space—as bees in early summer in sunlight in the flowering fields hum at their work. I love to stand in front of it and look at all the men killing one another in all the ways that men can kill one another. I also like to bring aspects of my home out into nature. There's a gorgeous cave where I plan to take pious and duty-bound Aeneas for a romantic picnic. He seems really happy here."

Frances Hodgson Burnett, The Secret Garden

MISTRESS MARY'S MELANCHOLIC MANOR AND SECRET OUTDOOR SPACE

Name: Mary Lennox, once-bratty orphan who has rather improved in her demeanor

Location: Yorkshire, England, where the wind is always wutherin'

Size: Unknown, as the owner, Mr. Archibald Craven, spends most of his time wandering the earth in a vain attempt to escape his sorrows

Years lived in: Since Mary's champagne-drenched, deadbeat parents dropped dead of cholera in India and she was unceremoniously shipped back to England; owned

MISTRESS MARY was surprised to find herself the newest resident of Misselthwaite Manor, a great, big, desolate old house surrounded by moors characterized by heather, gorse, broom, and the projected, aristocratic self-pity of its human inhabitants.

"Moors are the most depressing landscapes that exist," explains the housekeeper, Mrs. Medlock. "Their charm derives from their ability to make people want to kill themselves and others."

Mary, who also goes by "Mistress Mary," is growing accustomed to daily life in this decaying old pile of stone. Although she misses her Ayah's stories—which were just one of the many delights of living in a country that England decided to claim for itself—she has striven to embrace her life at the Manor.

"I have learned a lot here, including how to dress myself without pitching a fit," she says. "I have a capsule wardrobe now."

Misselthwaite features one hundred locked rooms, fires in hearths, the sound of crying in the corridors, a portrait gallery of dead children, and doors to the outside, which no one ever opens. The property also boasts a private walled garden that Mr. Craven locked up ten years ago after his beautiful wife fell from a tree branch and died, as a surprising number of people do in literature.

For Mary, this brown and dry outdoor space was a design challenge, and she has been working to refurbish it.

"The neighbors were threatening to file a complaint with the city about the garden," she says. "They kept leaving aggressive notes about maintaining our property. Total asshats."

And her labors have paid off. Mary has found that her low spirits have been improved by the now-vibrantly-alive garden's life-force of bees, butterflies, green twigs, roses, and ivy.

"A magical robin found a half-buried key and let me in," she says. "It was very queer."

A CHAT WITH MARY

HER STYLE

Because I'm only a child, I'm still developing my interior design aesthetic. But I like Misselthwaite's four-poster beds; ancient, handsome furniture; and snow-covered lawns with bunnies. And my mother used to always say that you can never overdo it with brocade, velvet, and the subjection of those who work for you.

IMPORTANT INFLUENCES

My young housemaid, Martha, has helped me to figure out my own place in the Manor and my taste. She doesn't really have any taste of her own as she's an unnecessarily chipper common servant, but when she was covered in soot the other morning, I thought: That is *exactly* the color I have been looking for to re-cover the chaise in my room.

HER INSPIRATION

I was found alone but alive in my old house in India after everyone else had left, so I would say that trauma and neglect really inform how I think about a room.

KEY FEATURES

There's an "Indian Room" here at the Manor where I can amuse myself with ivory elephants that look a lot like the actual elephants that were killed to make the ivory ones. Colonialism is not just a major injustice; it's also a major influence on décor.

IMPORTANT PIECES

Mr. Craven has an armchair in which he likes to sit and contemplate how life has been far crueler to him than anyone else on the planet. He doesn't pay much attention to the house. I thought that maybe he would incorporate some things from all the places he has traveled, but when I asked him about it, he told me to go sit in a closet.

MOST QUEER FEATURE

Probably Colin, the pale but ultimately perfectly healthy boy I found locked in a room. He had been in there his whole life and was convinced that he was going to die. When we met, he mostly just read picture books and acted like an entitled, self-pitying douche, but then we started to have this childhood-sexual-awakening thing going on, and I took him to the garden and healed him with flowers.

WHAT FRIENDS SAY

Well, Colin says he's going to live forever now, so that's going to be a disappointment. And he has this idea that when he grows up, he'll lecture about the Magic of the garden and make great scientific discoveries, and I'm like, Great—I'm the one who took you to the garden, and when I grow up, I'll probably just get married.

BIGGEST EMBARRASSMENT

All the men in the house used to believe that they were hunchbacks. How the hell does that happen?

PROUDEST DIY

I liked to gather daffydowndillys and arrange them in mason jars wrapped with little twine bows, but then Ben Weatherstaff told me that the mason jar thing is over.

BIGGEST CHALLENGE

Definitely bringing the garden and the Craven family back to life. Gardening isn't just about having dinner at Blue Hill at Stone Barns; it has a ton of metaphoric baggage.

PLANS FOR THE FUTURE

Dickon is talking to Glade about developing a home fragrance spray called Delicately Brimming Garden Air for their Limited Edition Spring Collection. He's also working on a line of paint called "Dickon for Sherwin-Williams" that includes "Frolicking Deer," "Mingling Blossoms," "Solemnity of Eggs," "Swelling Buds," and "Luscious Lily Pad."

Incorporate a lot of houseplants for a funky, outdoorsy vibe. Houseplants are currently enjoying a bit of a moment, and they'll definitely soften up an airy, loftlike space or a scullery maid's vermin-infested hovel. Maybe cover an accent wall in some Farrow & Ball wallpaper in a nice leaf print. I'd also suggest mixing textures—don't be afraid to hang a Renaissance tapestry next to a medieval tapestry in a playful convergence. I know this seems crazy, but trust me. I may be a kid, but I know a lot about tapestries.

DECORATING WITH CANDIDE

"One should cultivate one's garden. If you're French, maybe this garden has some grass that you're not allowed to walk on. Or perhaps it has some pigeons that fly at your head. Whatever the situation, don't be a lazy shit. Cultivate it."

INTERLUDE:
UNDERWATER LIVING

———

Don't be limited by living on land: It may be better down where it's wetter. Aquatic living offers creative spaces, including caves and lairs that are far from the maddening crowd. The sea witch in *The Little Mermaid* and Grendel's mother have perfected the art of monstrous female power, bloodlust, and decorating with starfish.

SEA WITCH: The best thing about underwater living is the complete control you have over your space.

GRENDEL'S MOTHER: I couldn't agree more.

SEA WITCH: No husband with his wagon-wheel coffee table.

GRENDEL'S MOTHER: God help us. It's exhausting to be an archetypal villain. You need a place to unwind. A place that is really yours.

SEA WITCH: Yes. With mollusks.

GRENDEL'S MOTHER: Absolutely. A place that is far better than what those heroes have on land. Hrothgar has his mead hall, Heorot, the hall of halls. He doles out rings and torques at the table. Who needs torques? Keep your damn torques, Hrothgar.

SEA WITCH: I have been perfectly fine without torques.

GRENDEL'S MOTHER: And the mead hall isn't all it's cracked up to be. No real sense of *hygge*.

SEA WITCH: I think that turned out not to be a thing, *hygge*.

GRENDEL'S MOTHER: Oh. Shame. Pleasant idea. They like benches, those warriors. Horns on the walls. Iron-braced doors. But those doors do nothing to keep out my Grendel, fiend from hell that he is.

SEA WITCH: What a fiend.

GRENDEL'S MOTHER: He is a wrecker of mead benches, rampaging among foes.

SEA WITCH: I do love a good rampage.

GRENDEL'S MOTHER: And those mead benches weren't so great anyway. Just a bunch of boring benches. If you're going to go with benches, I think you want one on one side of the table and some chairs on the other. To provide balance and contrast.

SEA WITCH: As an antagonist does for a protagonist.

GRENDEL'S MOTHER: Precisely.

SEA WITCH: That hall really isn't what it could be. Hrothgar should have gone with a light gray paint that reflects the light. Think Scandinavian, Hrothgar!

GRENDEL'S MOTHER: No taste. Now, my place—in the swamp—is a different matter. The water burns.

SEA WITCH: It's so unique to live in a fen.

GRENDEL'S MOTHER: The location is ideal. You take a left where the whale road forks.

SEA WITCH: Ah, yes.

GRENDEL'S MOTHER: That brainless hunk of meat Beowulf calls it a "hellish turn-hole," but nothing could be further from the truth.

SEA WITCH: He doesn't understand your influences.

GRENDEL'S MOTHER: True. I'm influenced by Cain, ogres, elves, and evil phantoms.

SEA WITCH: I have always admired your great sea beasts that attack with their tusks and tear at the chain mail of heroes. *Heroes.* Dime a dozen, those guys.

GRENDEL'S MOTHER: Thank you. I thought the sea beasts were a nice touch.

SEA WITCH: I also wanted my place to be different from the style of the mermaids. In their world, the water's as blue as the petals of the loveliest cornflower and as clear as the purest glass; and there are trees and plants growing down there, with stalks and leaves that bend so easily that they stir at the very slightest movement of the water, as though they were alive.

GRENDEL'S MOTHER: Good for them.

SEA WITCH: Yeah. The sea king has a palace made of coral with living flowers growing out of the walls and a roof made of cockleshells. I think he went overboard with the cockleshells—the key with cockleshells is restraint, am I right?

GRENDEL'S MOTHER: Absolutely. Cockleshells and pearls. What's the big deal? Why the obsession with pearls? They're just shiny sand.

SEA WITCH: The royal family has their great ballroom, too, with the walls and ceiling made of glass and a bunch more shells. Of course, my inspiration is rather different. My domain is on the far side of the roaring whirlpools, where no flowers and no sea grass grow and there's nothing but a bare, gray sandy bottom stretching right up to the whirlpools. I also have some delightful bubbling mud.

GRENDEL'S MOTHER: Don't forget the animal skeletons . . .

SEA WITCH: Yes. And some fat water snakes. Some polyps. Maybe a toad or two. My house is built of the bones of human folk who have been wrecked.

GRENDEL'S MOTHER: What are you going to do? Just waste all those perfectly good bones?

SEA WITCH: No way. Bones are not only accent pieces; they can be the basis for your whole design. I arranged them like Lincoln Logs. A femur here, a tibia there.

GRENDEL'S MOTHER: I may just have to Single White Female you on that one.

SEA WITCH: Do! It's an intimidating look. I need to make an impression on the idiot mermaids who come to see me. The king's youngest daughter popped by for a visit a little while back. I assumed that she wanted to admire my amazing bone house, but she was in love with a handsome prince with large dark eyes. And she wanted an immortal soul.

GRENDEL'S MOTHER: Of course she did.

SEA WITCH: Her skin was as clear and delicate as a roseleaf, and her eyes were as blue as the deepest lake.

GRENDEL'S MOTHER: Ugh. Double ugh.

SEA WITCH: Ugh is right. So I cut out her tongue and gave her a potion to transform her tail into legs. In the end, her prince married someone else, and she was turned into sea foam. *Sea foam.* I mean, that was good.

GRENDEL'S MOTHER: Classic.

SEA WITCH: I figured that if I don't even get a name, I should at least get some lovely new sea foam for my living room.

GRENDEL'S MOTHER: Yeah, we *don't* have names. What a bunch of bullshit.

VI.

COTTAGES, CABINS, AND HOVELS

Sir Gawain and the Green Knight

THE GREEN KNIGHT'S GREEN HOME OF FECUND FECUNDITY

Name: The Green Knight, pagan fertility spirit-slash-Christian knight who resembles the Jolly Green Giant but does not sell frozen vegetables

Location: Romantic

Size: Sort of epic

Years lived in: Time is cyclical and not linear, so who knows

FOR MANY OF US, the word "chapel" brings to mind a small building for Christian worship, perhaps attached to a main house. But if you're a veritably verdant knight, a conventional crap chapel is simply not going to do. Working with his decorator Joseph Campbell, the Green Knight devised a lovely burial mound.

"You would think that I would have some sort of palace that makes the Emerald City look like a dump," he says. "But I wanted something different. Something that might confuse people."

With its living wall and array of funky planters teeming with succulents, his natural home is suited to small-scale hosting and single combat. A game room is dedicated to tests of various sorts. There is a closet filled with board games (Risk and Candy Land are favorites), as well as an all-natural bar with wheatgrass infusions and carbonated spring water on tap.

"I always say that you can tell a lot about a person by how he plays games," he says. "We all have that friend who gets super-competitive and embarrasses you. Not honorable behavior at all."

And because he is a most massive man, the mightiest of mortals, green living is important to the Green Knight.

"Rich people who don't understand the concept of a baby have all-white nurseries," he says. "Well, in a similar vein, I'm green, so I have this all-green chapel or mound or whatever. My style reflects my personality, which you might call culturally hybrid."

The Green Knight's approach to decorating is tactile: He always starts by thinking about materials, whether that means selecting outdoor accessories from Smith & Hawken or picking up bags of soil at the Garden Center at the Home Depot. He favors a combination of the luxe and the natural, which he describes as "otherworldly."

"I had ceramic-tile floors from Armstrong installed as I don't wear shoes," he says. "The tile feels pleasantly cold under my feet. And I like sumptuous materials: white fur, burnished and beaten gold, silk, beauteous stones—maybe some butterflies, flowers, and bugs. Embroidery. Things that glimmer and glint. Things that make me want to speak alliteratively."

But there are always challenges to setting up your home if you're a threatening monster-knight capable of holding your own head in your hand. You need a place to stable your steed of pure green stock. You need sufficient storage for your green armor. And the Green Knight finds that he is away from home more than he would like.

"The neighbors get stroppy when I leave on a quest and don't tell them," he says. "And I mean real quests, not this *Eat Pray Love* nonsense. They say they would prefer to know when I'm gone, for the security of the neighborhood. And I'm like: I have to deal with Sir Gawain. Do you have to deal with Sir Gawain? Then they look sort of confused and leave me alone."

A CHAT WITH THE GREEN KNIGHT

HIS STYLE

You might say "bohemian." As any questing knight knows, the outside world is hostile and threatening. If you're not encountering some sort of wild beast, you're probably running into a dragon—or riding through a landscape onto which all sorts of human emotions have been projected. This means that you need a comfortable domestic space. I like crevices and crags. If you can incorporate some elements that suggest the diabolical, that's great, too.

HIS INSPIRATION

Definitely myself. And the natural world because I sort of, you know, embody that. Nothing should be too neat: Let things get a bit overgrown, if only to intimidate questing knights. I also take inspiration from bloated American suburban living. My largeness has the unfortunate effect of limiting my furniture options—most pieces are simply not big enough for me. But I find that Pottery Barn has some comfy options for sectionals. And the coffee tables at Restoration Hardware seem to have been *designed* for giants.

IMPORTANT INFLUENCES

Definitely forests. Dirt. Any kind of mound. And wood is very important to me. Natural materials. I have an aversion to off-gassing.

BEST FEATURE

I would say all my plants. I want my home to be like a greenhouse. A lush, green home filled to the brim with plants is absolutely dreamy. I like ferns, jade plants, and ivy. Fiddle-leaf figs and mother-in-law's tongue are nice, too. Those are plants: not fruit or body parts. I like plants that cascade. Tendrils. I was just saying to a knight the other day that you can never have

too many tendrils. I just let everything grow wild, and then you can wrap your tendrils around a nice garden bench—or yourself.

WHAT FRIENDS SAY

They love my terrariums. I know terrariums are everywhere these days, but they require a minimum of maintenance so I have plenty of time for riding and challenging knights to do stuff to prove their masculinity and worthiness.

BIGGEST EMBARRASSMENT

I can go a little over the top with greenery, but I *am* a pagan fertility spirit, as I believe I mentioned earlier, so whatever. I suggest at least ten plants per room, styled by Emily Henderson.

BIGGEST CHALLENGE

I decorate with an eye to the amount of sunlight in each room; I think about where all my plants should go in order to thrive. I need to think about temperature and water as well, of course. Some plants need misting. But my home is rather humid because, as I said, I'm a fertility spirit, so I'm pretty misty.

BIGGEST INDULGENCE

My green womb chair. I got it on sale at Design Within Reach. It was still a splurge. I thought that "Within Reach" meant that the chair would be cheap, but I think it just means that the store places the furniture physically within your reach.

PLANS FOR THE FUTURE

I'd like to incorporate more green paint, but there are so many color options: gray-green, blue-green, yellow-green. Do you want a green that is calming or energizing? A soft green or a bright green? Something that invokes moss or shady woods? Something that pairs well with blues, reds, corals, or browns? Or terra-cotta and rose? Benjamin Moore's "Aganthus Green 472" is a good all-around green. Pantone's "Young Wheat 12-0521" resembles lettuce, and Pratt & Lambert's "Clover 22-20" is excellent for shutters, molding, and window casings. Farrow & Ball's "Stone White 11" has a greenish-taupe undertone, and you can glaze it for more depth or whitewash it for a whole other quality. Anyway. Time to go on a quest.

DECORATING WITH ROBIN HOOD AND HIS MERRY MEN

"Our secret glen in Sherwood Forest is no Locksley Hall, but it's true to the soil of England and absolutely perfect for medieval glamping. We don't have yurts, but I sleep in the mouth of a cave. Our outlaw lifestyle is communal. We spend our days improving our proficiency at archery, playing at quarterstaff, and practicing smiting people. It won't surprise you that Maid Marian is quite crafty. If she's not lashing gray goose feathers onto arrow shafts, she's rising before the sun and having fine sport seeking out a deer. We don't need a lot of furniture, unlike all those lords, barons, bishops, abbots, and sheriffs—we have some fallen stumps. And we set up rough trestle tables with logs in lieu of stools, where we eat our great joints of roasted venison, wild boar, or horned beast and talk about what's new with the Crusades."

Fyodor Dostoyevsky, Crime and Punishment

RASKOLNIKOV'S DOMICILE OF DELIRIUM AND DISORDER

Name: Raskolnikov, a pale, shaky student who moves about like a drunkard and has been avoiding all forms of society, particularly of late

Location: St. Petersburg, Russia

Size: Like a cupboard or a trunk

Years lived in: Long enough to make some plans; rented by pawning an old, flat silver watch with a steel chain and an engraving of a globe (practically worthless)

STUDENT LIVING isn't generally luxurious, but some students go the extra mile to design a space that says "tiny little cell." Raskolnikov's tall, five-story tenement building consists entirely of cramped apartments inhabited by all kinds of jobbers and people trying to make a living: tailors, locksmiths, cooks, Germans of various descriptions, prostitutes, petty clerks and the like. There are two courtyards you can dart in and out of and doorbells that make extremely annoying clanking sounds.

"I should warn you that I'm feeling bilious, short-tempered, and uncharitable today," he says.

Raskolnikov's snug room is situated right under the roof, and his landlady and maid live in a separate apartment on the floor below. When he leaves the building, he must walk past his landlady's kitchen, the door of which is nearly always wide open onto the stairs.

"Whenever I walk by, I have a strange feeling," he says in an absent-minded and reflective tone. "It's not about her choice of backsplash, which is too bold for the space, but more of a morbid sensation of fear."

His room is about six paces long and features grimy yellow wallpaper that is coming off the walls and a ceiling so low that anyone of slightly above-average height might bang his head against the plaster at any moment. There is no room for a billiards table.

Raskolnikov strives to avoid "incriminating evidence of bad taste" and "fatal blunders" in his décor, even when living on a tight budget. The room's defining feature is a big, ungainly sofa, which takes up practically the whole of one wall and half the width of the space. It was at one time upholstered in chintz, but it is now in rags and serves as his bed.

"In a small space, you want your furniture to serve multiple purposes. So this approach is much more practical than even a Murphy bed," he says, smiling an ironic smile. "Also, I just like rags."

Raskolnikov describes himself as having "withdrawn from everyone," which gives him extra time to survey his living quarters with repugnance. Because he prefers to focus on "the things that matter in life," he has completely given up tidying and sweeping his quarters, except on the odd occasion.

"The maidservant irritates me to the point of bile and convulsions," he mutters hastily. "And there's my landlady, always after me for the rent. She stripped and repainted some antique pieces in her apartment. I nearly lost it. Oh, what shameful things happen in the world nowadays."

A CHAT WITH THE
REMARKABLY HANDSOME RASKOLNIKOV

HIS STYLE

I like to keep things pared down and simple. People think that with student living, you need a poster of "The Kiss by the Hôtel de Ville," white twinkle lights, and a mini-fridge. But I'm not going to get a mini-fridge as I don't eat. So really, my furniture is commensurate with my surroundings: three old chairs, not in very good condition, and a painted table where I keep my exercise books, which are covered in dust because I don't exercise because what's the point. Lord in heaven!

IMPORTANT INFLUENCES

Crushing poverty. Something along the lines of *La Bohème*, but without the pretty music. I'm also influenced by a tense, irritable state of mind that verges on hypochondria. Fear. Oh, and tortoises. I want my home to be like a tortoise withdrawing into its shell.

HIS INSPIRATION

I'm inspired by things that make my heart stand still, and by a terrible sense of disorder that affects my whole being and makes me feel like I'm going to lose control of myself, so I try to fasten my attention on something, think about something, anything at all. I suppose that if I'm going to be spending all this time at home, I could throw myself into some home improvements. I could do something with cinder blocks, maybe a design project that says "industrial chic" rather than "cash-strapped student plagued by vicious contempt."

KEY FEATURES

Probably my Turkish sofa. What a joke. That sofa is about as Turkish as I am. I was contemplating the monstrous act of getting rid of it, but then I decided just to stay in and read an exhausting letter from my mother and not eat cabbage soup.

IMPORTANT PIECES

I have some accessories that make the space distinctive. A jug of vodka. And a hat that is rather conspicuous and absurd. Yes, probably too memorable.

It is one of those tall, round affairs from Zimmerman's, but now it's completely worn out and faded and covered in holes and stains and missing its brim. Maybe I should get a hat rack for it, something classy by Bentwood. Walnut. But for that, I suppose I would need money. And to be able to make a decision. I also have an axe.

BIGGEST CHALLENGE

You can really hear the footsteps in the hallways. In the name of heaven! And it's very much city living here, so there's also a lot of street noise, not to mention the stench from the little shops and drinking dens, and when you go outside, there is *so much sun*. I mean, why? It's like the sun is just showing off, or trying to be a pain in my ass, or something. But when I feel suffocated and claustrophobic, I sometimes go out in the street, as if I'm taking a walk, just for show. It's repugnant, but going back to my room is still more repugnant. God, I use the word "repugnant" a lot, don't I?

BEST DIY

Nothing yet, but I have a plan. An undertaking. I cannot think where I have got so much cunning.

BEST ADVICE

For god's sake, come up with a nighttime ritual. It's important to end the day in a way that calms your nervous tremors. I sleep on my sofa just as I am, without bothering to undress, without a sheet, covering myself with my old, threadbare student's coat and resting my head on a single small pillow beneath which I put all the linen I possess, clean and soiled, to give some extra height. You might say that the rags on my sofa-bed are not unlike the rags and tatters of vague thoughts that swarm in my head. Maybe I'll take Lunesta.

PLANS FOR THE FUTURE

I'd rather not say.

DECORATING CHALLENGES WITH DOCTOR FAUSTUS

"There's a certain amount of pressure to host Mephistopheles in style, and he has been coming here a lot lately. My study is truly a magical place. You'll find a large box, a globe, a cross, and a lot of books. I have the usual suspects—Aristotle and Justinian and the *Iliad* and stuff like that—but I like to display my necromantic books as they really embody my overreaching and transgressive desires. And I'll be damned if I'm going to have some dull study like all the dime-a-dozen scholarly drones out there. I'm thinking about drawing a circle on the floor: something with some symbols. Maybe I'll conjure Helen of Troy, too. She would be a nice addition to the room. Very, very pretty, they say."

Jane Austen, Sense and Sensibility

THE DASHWOODS' CASUAL AND TOLERABLY COMFORTABLE COTTAGE

Names: Elinor Dashwood, responsible eldest sister, daughter, and heroine, who demonstrates strength of understanding and coolness of judgment, even when people are real jerkwads; plus her mother, Mrs. Dashwood, and two sisters, Marianne and Margaret

Location: Devonshire, England

Size: Comfortable and compact, with four bedrooms, two garrets, offices, unhandsome stairs, and two sixteen-square-foot sitting rooms (too cramped for parties, obviously), which is just another way of saying *really disappointingly small*

Years lived in: For several months, since leaving the family's *enormo* Sussex estate of Norland Park, where for many generations the Dashwoods had lived in so respectable a manner as to engage the general good opinion of their surrounding acquaintance (so that was nice of them); rented

DEATH IS A REAL BUMMER under most circumstances, but it's a particular bummer when it means that you get kicked out of your house. Such was the situation for Elinor Dashwood; her sisters, Marianne and Margaret; and their mother, Mrs. Dashwood, upon the death of their beloved father and husband.

Norland Park was passed to the sisters' half-brother, John (thanks, patriarchy), and his highly unpleasing wife, Fanny, immediately set to work alienating all the Dashwood women and forcing them from the premises.

"John is not an ill-disposed young man, unless to be rather cold-hearted and rather selfish is to be ill-disposed," says Elinor. "You know, just as I'm saying this, I'm realizing that *it totally is.*"

Luckily, the Dashwoods received a letter in the true spirit of friendly accommodation from Sir John Middleton, who offered them a cottage on his estate of Barton Park, four miles northward of Exeter. Although the Dashwoods were unfamiliar with the area, they tried to see their banishment from Norland as an opportunity for a new real estate adventure.

Devonshire is known for its rich pastures, downs, pleasant woods, and total lack of beaux.

"The weather was nice when we arrived, which cheered us up, as did our three lovely servants, which is the number of servants you have when you're poor," says Elinor. "But then the reality of our diminished marriage prospects started to dawn on us, and I'm not going to lie: We really over-did it on tea that evening. Marianne had a terrible tea headache the next morning."

Barton Cottage has a neat wicket gate, and a small green court is the whole of its demesne in front. "Demesne" derives from the Old French *demeine*, and ultimately from the Latin *dominus*, which translates as, "Feudalism is still a thing, so none of this shit belongs to you."

Friends have been quick to offer decorating advice, as well as effusive praise of the kind of house that they themselves will never be required to inhabit.

"Willoughby loves the place," says Elinor. "He suggested that we hang a white plastic faux stag mount on the wall, but we told him that we needed the money for flour and socks."

A CHAT WITH ELINOR

HER STYLE

I esteem funky, mismatched drawer pulls from Anthropologie, distressed stools, and flour-sack tea towels. I think very highly of dishes that are designed to look like they *already* have crazing on them. Honestly, I just do what *Apartment Therapy* tells me to do.

IMPORTANT INFLUENCES

Rain is a big influence. It rains a lot here, so we have plenty of time to stay in and think about what kinds of window coverings would be best and how many more cushions we need to embroider. Marianne is always taking walks in the rain. I swear, one day she's going to get really sick in a flushed, sweaty, erotic way, and I'm going to be like, I told you the rain was bad.

INTERESTING FEATURES

Our rent is uncommonly moderate, which is great, but when we moved in, the cottage was lacking *all* the cottage things: a tiled roof, green window shutters, and honeysuckle. It's like the Middletons had never read a single blog about charming cottages. I don't know what the hell they do with their time.

HER INSPIRATION

Not shabby chic. Ugh. It looks like you ate a bunch of pink roses and then vomited them up. *Oh, a cottage! How shabby chic!*, everyone says. If I have to hear that phrase one more time, I swear I'm just going to stop making polite conversation.

IMPORTANT PIECES

We received some nice gifts from people who are supposedly our friends. Charlotte Palmer and Mrs. Jennings got us a serpentine front chest *and* a serpent. Lucy Steele sent us a mahogany chair with a Georgian splat. I mean, what the hell is a splat?

KEY FEATURES

Not a horse, I can tell you that. We don't have a friggin' horse.

BIGGEST SPLURGE

Marianne was pretty excited about the Marimekko line at Target, but I told her that we could only get one tray. We really haven't budgeted for Finnish trays.

MOST ROMANTIC FEATURE

Probably our total isolation (#pastoral). I could say a lot more about the prospect of the cottage and the picturesque—a lot more—but I won't.

WHAT FRIENDS SAY

Everyone keeps referring to the cottage as our "beach house," but we don't have lobster-printed flip-flops or a monogramed L.L. Bean Boat and Tote bag or anything. Honestly, we don't receive a lot of visitors because it's a challenge to feed them, but sometimes Colonel Brandon comes by for a half hour and sits and doesn't talk.

PROUDEST DIY

We sort of DIYed almost everything, so it's hard to say. Maybe setting up Marianne's pianoforte? It was a real pain to fit it into our sitting room, but the music does help to fill the endless hours of waiting for Edward to grace us with his presence. On the days when there's nothing to do, we just walk around, taking our aprons on and off.

BIGGEST EMBARRASSMENT

The walls still need some embellishment. I want to start an art collection as I'm rather artistic myself, but not in a way that would make me not want to be a wife. Right now, we just have a lot of my drawings up on the walls, but I'd like a piece by Man Ray or Lucian Freud, once we can afford sugar.

BIGGEST CHALLENGE

Sir John is always stopping by to drop off a nice side of animal, but these cuts can be hard to cook as we don't have our Le Creuset Dutch oven anymore. Fanny insisted that it stay at Norland. She is *so* deficient in natural taste.

PLANS FOR THE FUTURE

We're keen to make some improvements because that's what you do when you have a house in the nineteenth century. Marianne would like her own nook where she can read Cowper and Scott in the afternoons, and I'd like a military-grade bunker where I can go to escape all the crap that everyone constantly dumps on me. Did I ask you to tell me your dirty little secrets? Most of the time, I just want a stiff cup of tea.

BEST ADVICE

Consider familial and collective responsibility over individual feeling when it comes to selecting paint colors, especially if you want to paint a room a glamorous glossy black, which Marianne really did think would work. And don't get discouraged. Am I sometimes a wee bit melancholy about our lack of patterned poufs and marriage prospects? Sure. But we'll probably do surprisingly well in the latter department because we're heroines in a Jane Austen novel. And when it comes to patterned poufs, well: I've known a few of those in my day, and her name begins with *Lucy Steele*.

HOW TO SURVIVE YOUR FATHER'S TERRIBLE TASTE WITH ANNE ELLIOT

"My father, Sir Walter, is a foolish, spendthrift baronet who has not the principle or sense enough to maintain himself in the situation in which Providence placed him. And he really likes mirrors. He hangs them up *absolutely everywhere*. I may have lost my bloom, but not my appreciation of the absurd."

Johann David Wyss, The Swiss Family Robinson

Names: Father (William); his resourceful little wife, Elizabeth; sons Fritz, Ernest, Jack, and Franz; and dogs Turk and Juno (plus monkey Nip and jackal Fangs)

Location: Thirty feet above the ground on a desert island, not far from Prospect Hill, Cape Disappointment, and Jackal River

Size: Much bigger than the tree house you had as a kid

Years lived in: Almost a decade; neither owned nor rented as private property does not exist outside "civilization"

AFTER MANY DAYS of being tempest-tossed by a raging storm, the Swiss Family Robinson was cast onto a richly vegetated but unidentified and rather confusingly geographically characterized island (possibly near the equator). While some people in this position would have despaired, Father wasn't having any of that. He describes his life philosophy as "all about work."

"Just because you are stranded on a desert island doesn't mean you should sit around with this season's beach read," he says. "No, siree. We're all about labor in this family. Staying busily employed. Work brings you closer to the divine. Work is how great nations are born, especially great nations that are all about subjugating other nations."

Initially, the sun beat burningly the livelong day on their bare rocky spot, and their only shelter was a poor tent, beneath the canvas of which the heat was even more oppressive than on the open shore. They began to wonder: Why should they not accomplish something useful and exchange their melancholy and unwholesome abode for a pleasant shady dwelling-place that would improve their health and spirits?

"We feared that we were lost, but really it was an opportunity to start fresh and build our dream house: a place that not only provides comfort and shelter, but also represents order and perseverance in the face of hardship," he says.

The result is Falconhurst, a tree-house abode contrived among the branches. It is the safest and most charming home in the world.

"As we all know," Father says, "a remodeling project can really put a strain on a marriage. But my wife shows such fortitude and foresight. And prudence. I was worried about perching and roosting like birds, but she assured me that she had seen a home in Switzerland that was up among the branches of a lime tree, with a strong floor and a staircase to reach it. And so I told her that I would seriously consider her idea, and she said, 'I'm so goddamn grateful to you for that,' which is nice as gratitude is an important virtue."

The family was able to outfit Falconhurst with provisions from the wreck, including a service of silver plate and a cellaret of good old wine. When they looked over the stores, they found a large stock of knives and forks, kitchen utensils of all sorts, potted meats, portable soups, Westphalian hams, sausages, a bag of maize and wheat, a quantity of other seeds and vegetables, peas, oats, wheat, seeds, and young fruit trees (only apple, pear, chestnut, orange, almond, peach, apricot, plum, and cherry). They were also fortunate to come across a cow, a donkey, two goats, six sheep, a ram, and a fine sow, as well as ducks, geese, and pigeons. Nails, an axe, a hammer, pincers, chisels, and augers helped with the construction of the house, and agricultural implements, lanterns, a barrel of sulfur for matches, guns, shot belt, powder flasks, bullets, ironmongery, plumber's tools, lead, paint, grindstones, cart wheels, spades and plowshares, and a telescope also came in handy.

"Nature provides for all things," says Father. "But I guess we did get some things from the ship, too."

The family put in natural wide-plank bamboo flooring throughout and also incorporated bamboo in some accessories, including picture frames, although they don't have any pictures to put in them.

"Bamboo is a lovely material. It's also environmentally friendly, which is a value that is quite important here in New Switzerland as we're not sure if we'll ever get back to Old Switzerland."

A CHAT WITH FATHER

THEIR STYLE

Ship chic meets tiki, with a soupçon of colonialism, although we haven't found any savages. It is important to control the natural world, to transform nature's bounty into useful things that make your life more comfortable and meaningful. There's no limit to what a man can do! And by that I really do mean *a man*. We're very into salvaging: Reuse everything, I always say. We salvaged much of our furniture from the captain's room onboard the ship. Most of it is in the style of Thomasville's Ernest Hemingway Collection. We also found doors and window frames, with their bolts, bars, and locks, which was nice as houses need doors to keep out savages, if they are about.

IMPORTANT INFLUENCES

Society. I mean, you don't want to leave behind all the great things that society offers just because you're on a desert island. What would my wife do if she couldn't wash and sew and cook for us? And what would I do if I couldn't shoot things and dispense parables and wisdom to my sons? Yes, society has it all figured out.

INTERESTING FEATURES

We have a number of officers' chests from the ship, as well as those that belonged to the carpenter and gunsmith. One chest was filled with fancy goods, including gold and silver watches, snuffboxes, buckles, studs, chains, rings, and all manner of trinkets. I don't know what the hell we're supposed to do with this stuff now as we're outside a capitalist system that imbues commodities with value, but I guess we can just look at them. We have also taken advantage of local materials to create some unique pieces. My wife contrived a raffia coffee table and styled it with a dish of sea glass, a conch shell, and some flamingo feathers. Although there weren't any Don Featherstone pink plastic flamingos on the ship, we do have the real thing, and I have taught my sons to shoot them, which is a useful life skill.

INSPIRATION

Our use of rattan is influenced by *The Golden Girls*. Rattan is delightful. A magazine stand is always nice, although of course we don't have any magazines. We have a rattan shelf where we have displayed our family collection of turtle shells. My wife also speedily contrived rattan headboards and end tables for us all, so we have quite the bedroom sets now. Rattan is the essence of bohemian-chic living, but you don't want to go overboard. HA! Get it? *Overboard?* That's a really great film, too.

IMPORTANT PIECES

My wife improvised a dining-room table of a board laid on two casks, and on this was spread a white damask tablecloth. The table is an excellent place for refreshment, repose, and most tempting repasts of boiled iguana or salted kangaroo. She is quite a cook—she's always making tureens of soup and capital omelets, along with Dutch cheese and slices of ham, butter and biscuits, and bottles of canary wine. She is so resourceful. I suppose I could have let her do this interview, but as the head of the household and moral guide of my family, I prefer to do the talking.

BIGGEST SPLURGE

A vigilant cock that wakes us in the morning.

WHAT FRIENDS SAY

Well, maybe one day a ship will show up, and we can ask them what they think.

PROUDEST DIY

Well, we're the DIY family. No one DIYs like we do. And DIYing requires patience, which is an important virtue. Take driftwood. Driftwood is all the rage here, and you can do anything with it. My dear wife arranged some coconut bowls on the open driftwood shelves in the kitchen, next to a pelican beak and the head of a penguin.

BIGGEST EMBARRASSMENT

We had very limited options with textiles: just the ship's sails. So the house is mostly done in a clean white. But we did incorporate the occasional pop of color with some animal skins—one from a tiger, which is a common tropical animal—and some ikat prints. You may think that ikat is over, but nothing is over on a desert island.

BIGGEST CHALLENGE

We could use more storage for weapons. On one trip back to the ship, we added three excellent guns, as well as a whole armful of swords, daggers, and knives. You can never have too many weapons.

PLANS FOR THE FUTURE

Just to rise up betimes and, after a hearty prayer for God's blessing, set to work.

BEST ADVICE

I love giving advice—wisdom, really. First, avoid travel by ship. Second, if you must travel by ship, make sure that the ship is well stocked. And third, maybe just don't travel.

HOW TO PITCH A TENT ON A DESERT ISLAND WITH ROBINSON CRUSOE

"A flat of green is best for tent pitching, and you will no doubt find lots of these on your island as there is really nothing on desert islands apart from land. Ideally, you want a larger tent to preserve you from the rains and a smaller tent within, covered with a tarpaulin saved from the shipwreck you have just experienced. Poles and sails are fine tent materials. I also recommend a good fence to keep you from being devour'd by wild beasts. I also opted to make a cave just behind my tent, which served me like a cellar to my house. It cost me a lot of labor, but it was a good scheme as I could store my bags and boxes of gunpowder there. And I didn't really have anything else to do. Being left entirely destitute of all comfort and company really allows you a lot of time for home improvements."

D. H. Lawrence, Lady Chatterley's Lover

CONNIE AND CLIFFORD'S WAR-RAVAGED FAMILY SEAT PLUS HUT IN THE WOODS

Names: Constance Chatterley, a bonny Scotch trout of a lady, and Clifford Chatterley, a baronet and member of the intelligentsia

Location: In the soulless ugliness of the coal-and-iron Midlands

Size: Massive enough for Connie to conduct an affair in her third-floor parlor without much trouble

Years lived in: Since the autumn of 1920, after the end of all the death and horror (the pity of war, etc.); owned

OURS IS ESSENTIALLY a tragic decorating age, so we refuse to take it tragically. The cataclysm has happened, we are among the ruins, we start to build up new little habitats, to have new little hopes of reorganizing our closets and drawers.

This is more or less Connie's position.

"The war really brought the roof down over my head," she says. "So we had to have it repaired, and it's so effing expensive to repair a roof."

Roofing is only one of the many challenges that Connie has faced at Wragby Hall, but she's more than prepared to handle the ins and outs of domestic life at her husband's family seat. This long low old house in brown stone was begun about the middle of the eighteenth century, and added onto, till it was a warren of a place without much distinction. But the property boasts a number of sheep.

Sir Clifford hadn't expected to inherit Wragby, but his older brother, Herbert, was killed in 1916, and his pale and tense father, Sir Geoffrey, had the decency to die of chagrin shortly thereafter. The home is filled with carefully curated antiques, dusty old books, and a pervasive sense of post-war doom regarding the future of England's aristocracy, which readers will recognize from *Downton Abbey*.

Wragby also benefits from the charming artisanal culture of the region: sooty, underpaid men who are lowered into dangerous mines. Connie isn't a fan of the pit or the rows of wretched, small, begrimed brick houses in the nearby Tevershall Village.

"I don't like to go into town because it's gross," she says. "Sometimes Sir Clifford has to go for business, but mostly he just sits in the breakfast nook we added, reading his newspapers and trying not to think about severed body parts."

Sir Clifford came back from the war a "changed man," which is totally a thing in war novels. But Connie and Sir Clifford keep their spirits up by attending Clarissa Dalloway's parties in London and hosting Sir Clifford's cronies regularly.

"Sometimes I string up fairy lights in the backyard, and we throw a couple of pheasants on the grill," says Connie. "But my god, those flannel-trousers Cambridge men do go on and on about Racine and Bolshevism."

The property also includes a charming gamekeeper's hut surrounded by a pervy landscape of dandelions, daisies, and the lush, dark green of hyacinths.

"I can tell you about the hut, too," she says. "Few people will be able to get their hands on the unexpurgated version of the novel until after the obscenity trial anyway. Ah, I do love those orange-and-white Penguin covers. Ours will have a phoenix on it, which is fabulous."

A CHAT WITH CONNIE

THEIR STYLE

I enjoy blazing fires, fluffy beds, paintings of the Scottish countryside, and anything with a sturdy, energetic, country-girl vibe that pushes back against the messy sterility of modern life. Sir Clifford's taste runs to etched crystal decanters, German reproductions of Cézanne and Renoir, and an heir to the estate produced by my boning another man.

IMPORTANT INFLUENCES

Sir Clifford is influenced by the quirky and offbeat design features of the trenches, such as rotting corpses, rats, lice, and overflowing latrines. Not that he wants those things! He'd just like to be sure that such an approach doesn't figure into our redecorating choices. And I get it; trenches are narrow and icky, and they flood all the time.

FAVORITE ELEMENT

For Sir Clifford, probably our housekeeper, who is a dried-up, elderly, superlatively correct female I tend to avoid. For myself, I love Wragby's woods, which are a remnant of the great forest where Robin Hood hunted— I mean, Merrie Olde England is such a brilliant idea. Sometimes when I feel restless, I rush off across the park and lie prone in the bracken. Bracken is a vascular plant from the genus of large, coarse ferns in the family *Dennstaedtiaceae*, and that shit is all over the property.

UNIQUE ELEMENTS TO THE GROUNDS

Definitely the gamekeeper's hut, which is like a backyard retreat, but without a gazing globe or garden gnomes. Mellors keeps it awfully nice, and it has been an escape from the evil electric lights and diabolical rattlings of engines, as well as a place of ridiculous postures and acts, or so the narrator says, but he also says a lot about my haunches.

BEST FEATURES OF THE HUT

Mellors has the nicest way of arranging blankets on the floor for when we bone, and he always hangs his gun up on the wall so it's not liable to just, you know, go off. And he has a chicken coop, where once he felt among an old hen's feathers and drew out a faintly peeping chick for me to hold. I tried to convince him to order a new chicken coop from Williams Sonoma that was built in Washington state from solid red cedar custom milled by a local, family-run sawmill, but he just said something about wanting to stroke my breasts and loins and to stop talking about Williams Sonoma.

FUTURE PLANS FOR THE HUT

The hut has shown me that it's great to have a place to really tune out the world—and to enjoy marvelous swoonlike caresses of my soft, warm buttocks, coming nearer and nearer to the very quick of me. Maybe one day, I'll also add an Airstream trailer to the property or even convert some shipping containers into a space of simplicity and virtue. Sir Clifford suggested a yurt in the style of Marie Antoinette's peasant village.

WHAT FRIENDS SAY

Mellors says, "Tha's got such a nice tail on thee. Tha's got the nicest arse of anybody. It's the nicest, nicest woman's arse as is! An' ivery bit of it is woman, woman sure as nuts. Tha'rt not one o' them button-arsed lasses as should be lads, are ter! Tha's got a real soft sloping bottom on thee, as a man loves in 'is guts. It's a bottom as could hold the world up, it is!" But you probably mean about the estate! I don't know. I haven't really asked. Who cares.

BIGGEST EMBARRASSMENT

Probably the sensual flame of passion pressing through my bowels, but not anymore! And it's embarrassing that you can see the chimney of Tevershall pit from our property, with its clouds of steam and smoke, as well as the raw struggle of the village, which begins at the gates and trails in utter hopeless ugliness for a long and gruesome mile. I think we may have to plant some tall ornamental shrubberies.

PROUDEST DIY

I find the portraits of Sir Clifford's ancestors a bit dreary, so I have been gradually replacing them with my own paintings of perky owls.

BIGGEST INDULGENCE

I would say the belief that the aristocracy could possibly endure, particularly in this absurd postwar wasteland. Otherwise, probably the new thirteen-thousand-dollar Chihuly anemone chandelier for the dining room.

BEST ADVICE

Get a small, kid-friendly farm somewhere, as Mellors and I plan to do. But for heaven's sake, don't let your kid's stuff take over the place, even if he's not in fact going to be the heir to a great estate. You need to designate adult spaces for adult activities such as running around naked in the rain with a dog. And nickname your genitals. That's always quite fun.

CONCLUSION:
WHAT THE BUTLER SAID

When you think of a great butler, he is bound, almost by definition, to be an Englishman. From polishing the silver to putting in trunk-calls to London, the butler keeps a great country estate running in an orderly manner. Beach of Blandings Castle and Frith of Manderley embody a professionalism that is rarely matched. Frith is downright efficient, and Beach is a really sound egg.

FRITH: Last night I dreamt I went to Manderley again.

BEACH: What?

FRITH: Nothing.

BEACH: Ah, these great houses. And our great English countryside. We are so lucky to be butlers.

FRITH: We are.

BEACH: Deuce of a long time I have been at the castle.

FRITH: Yes, deuce of a long time for me, too.

BEACH: Eighteen years have I served under his lordship's household, commencing as under-footman and rising to my present position.

FRITH: Indeed.

BEACH: And I'm much better than Jeeves.

FRITH: Or Merriman.

BEACH: Or Wadsworth.

FRITH: Indeed. Ours are such fine houses. And it's our responsibility to keep them in order. Not just for Mr. de Winter and Lord Emsworth, but for the public, too, as sad, normal people need something to aspire to and never, ever possibly attain because of fundamental social inequalities.

BEACH: Quite.

FRITH: When the rabble comes for tours, we always show them the long drawing room.

BEACH: The rabble loves a long drawing room. We have the rabble to visit for the August Bank Holiday, but his lordship does not enjoy this. He refers to it as "a miniature Inferno."

FRITH: Total anarchy in the marquee.

BEACH: Indeed. Of course, at Blandings, we like to keep the emphasis on the gardens. The main interest of Lord Emsworth's life is his garden. Flowers are a magnet for him. You see, he has one of those minds capable of accommodating but one thought at a time. He likes to take walks around the property and say things like "What the deuce!" and "How the dickens!" He's inspired by Kensington Gardens and by the flowers at the Savoy.

FRITH: The décor at the Savoy is nice.

BEACH: Indeed. The gardens at Blandings are at their loveliest in high summer. There is a summer stillness that hangs over the gardens of the castle. We are very big on summer stillness.

FRITH: As one would be.

BEACH: The gardens of Blandings Castle are that original garden from which we are all exiled. All those who know them long to return.

FRITH: Oh, you mean like the Bible.

BEACH: Yes, I mean like the Bible.

FRITH: I find the land around Manderley rather dramatic. The woods, always a menace, encroach upon the drive with long tenacious fingers. The beeches with white, naked limbs lean close to one another, their branches intermingled in a strange embrace, making a vault above like the archway in a church. When the sun sets, it leaves a glow upon the headland, and from the terrace you could hear the ripple of the coming tide washing in the little bay.

BEACH: That sounds intense.

FRITH: It is. The house is secretive and silent, gray stone shining in the moonlight. Gray stone that doesn't shine is unacceptable.

BEACH: A country estate with subpar, non-shiny gray stone is the worst.

FRITH: Yes. You want your house to be a thing of grace and beauty, exquisite and faultless.

BEACH: Our one fault is that the family does not possess a Family Curse.

FRITH: That's a problem.

BEACH: I know.

FRITH: You should quit. Posthaste.

BEACH: I am too faithful and observant. And Lord Emsworth is okay. His taste isn't bad. He's fond of the décor at the Senior Conservatives Club and the Regent Grill, where he enjoys a capital chop and half a bottle of claret from time to time. He's a tough old gentleman. Full of beans. He likes splendid things.

FRITH: How jolly.

BEACH: He did get really hung up about a gravel path once. And he cannot abide decorative gourds or pumpkins as seasonal décor as no Earl of Emsworth has ever won a first prize for pumpkins at the Shrewsbury Show.

FRITH: He feels that deeply?

BEACH: He does. It makes him sorer than a gumboil. But we find ways to incorporate fall-inspired colors elsewhere in the castle. Our amber drawing room is quite stunning. Amber is a lovely color. It's not just for freezing prehistoric dead things in time, you know.

FRITH: Certainly not. Amber has endless possibilities. Like Millennial Pink.

FRITH: Indeed.

BEACH: His lordship can be rather eccentric. At times, I find myself engaged in surprising duties. Once, his debt-ridden and mopey son Freddie brought a bag of rats to the castle, and I had to secure it.

FRITH: Rats add nothing to interior design. They are just gross rodents.

BEACH: And it is not, strictly, my place to carry rats, but a good butler is always ready to give and take. Only this way can the amenities of a large country estate be preserved.

FRITH: We understand that a butler should anticipate and answer all his employer's needs, but he should be careful not to exist as a human being. Truth be told, I have found the new Mrs. de Winter tricky. Much of the time, she eats alone. She has magnificent and utterly wasteful breakfasts. Breakfast is the most important meal of the day, particularly when you're facing yet another day of knowing that you do not measure up to a dead woman.

BEACH: True.

FRITH: Sometimes Mr. de Winter joins her for dinner. And then after dinner, they lounge in the library, the master reading his paper, and the second Mrs. de Winter brooding, her chin in her hands, thinking that she is not the first person to lounge

there in possession of the chair, and shivering, as though someone has opened the door behind her and let a draught into the room. Rebecca's chair, Rebecca's cushion, Rebecca's dog.

BEACH: That sounds depressing.

FRITH: It is. Mr. de Winter displays the greatest of all English aristocratic traits: loving your house more than your wife.

BEACH: Lord Emsworth is very fond of his pig, Empress. She resembles a captive balloon with ears and a tail and is as nearly circular as a pig can be without bursting.

FRITH: Sadly, we lack a pig. But there are so many other fine features to recommend Manderley. For example, the new Mrs. de Winter's bedroom is a lovely place to dress for dinner whilst trapped by an oppressive sense of your own inferiority.

BEACH: A room should always be large enough to hold your despair.

FRITH: Rebecca really did have the most marvelous taste. The west wing is unsurpassed.

BEACH: Is the new wife's room in the west wing?

FRITH: No. It's a lot lighter in the east wing, and the rooms look down across the lawns to the sea. It's true that the rooms in the west wing are bigger and have fine details like curtains that hide dead imprisoned moths, as well as the ornaments of a dead woman herded together in the center of the bed and left there, covered with a sheet. We love dustsheets at Manderley.

BEACH: There is a certain crispness to them.

FRITH: Linens are so important in a great estate. I cannot stand those stretchy T-shirt sheets. Horrible things.

BEACH: His lordship's bed is very important to him. As a general rule, he is an early and a sound sleeper. At present, he is trying out one of those new Purple mattresses. It seemed like a better option than Tuft & Needle, which I assumed was the name of a pub.

FRITH: Yes, I keep seeing these newfangled mattresses in my Facebook feed. They arrive in a box! Can you imagine?

BEACH: His lordship said that it was the most dashed strange thing he had ever seen. He is also fond of pillows. When he is distressed, he sinks back on his pillows. You know, people say that it's silly to spend a lot of money on your bed, but you spend eight hours a day in bed—or if you're an aristocrat, maybe fourteen. It's worth the expense.

FRITH: They lead tiring lives. As do we. Luckily I have the help of the housekeeper, Mrs. Danvers, who has a skull's face and skeleton's body.

BEACH: That sounds pleasant.

FRITH: Mrs. Danvers prefers to think of the house as an elaborate torture device for the new Mrs. de Winter. Take the graceful and fragile morning room, where Mrs. de Winter—the first one, you know, Rebecca—always did her correspondence and telephoning after breakfast. Of course, the new Mrs. de Winter didn't even know where it was. Walked right into the garden-room. But Mrs. Danvers says: What can you expect from a woman with no pedigree?

BEACH: Absolutely nothing.

FRITH: I swear. She doesn't understand simple things like which fires were lit in which room at which time of day. Even the dogs get that. She also sucks at approving menus. And she knocks over glasses of port.

BEACH: Lord.

BEACH: You know what I say? You can put flowers on the mantelpiece and sheets on the bed, but Rebecca is dead, buried in the crypt in the church with all the other dead de Winters. Or maybe not. Or whatever.

BEACH: I say get a pig.

FRITH: Farm animals are considered very charming on *House Hunters International*.

BEACH: Boom. Problem solved.

ACKNOWLEDGMENTS

THANK YOU to my wonderful editor David Cashion and to my agent, Jim McCarthy, and to everyone at Dystel, Goderich & Bourret. Thanks are also due to the design team at Abrams, including designer Darilyn Carnes; my publicist, Jordan Jacobson; and Kim Lew in marketing. I would also like to thank Becca Stadtlander for her beautiful illustrations. I feel so fortunate to have had the opportunity to collaborate with such a talented artist. This book began as a column for the Toast (RIP), and I am grateful to my fabulous editor Nicole Chung. Over the past few years, I have talked to a lot of people about famous houses in literature. A lot. So thank you to everyone who shared ideas or discussed the project with me, including Audra Abt, Laura Aull, Elizabeth Bearden, Rian Bowie, Anne Boyle, Kate Callahan, Jane Carr, Amy Catanzano, Erin Chapman, Jay Curley, Allison Devers, Lara Dodds, Michelle Dowd, Irina Dumitrescu, Eric Ekstrand, Meredith Farmer, Jon Farina, Jen Feather, Patricia Fels, Dean Franco, Sharon Fulton, Laura Giovanelli, Manda Goltz, Jennifer Greiman, Omaar Hena, Sarah Hogan, Jeff Holdridge, Erika Jaeggli, Melissa Jenkins, Kristina Kaufman, Catherine Keyser, Sarah Torretta Klock, Stephanie Koscak, Alison Kinney, Sara Landreth, Sarah Landreth, Cristina Marcelo, Sam Meyer, Patrick Moran, Anne Moyer, Francie Neukom, Kelly Neukom, Niamh O'Leary, Morna O'Neill, Adrienne Pilon, Jenny Pyke, Dan Quiles, Jenny Raab, Emily Richard, Jessica Richard, Anne Boyd Rioux, Joanna Ruocco, Jo Scutts, Carter Smith, Randi Saloman, Jeff Solomon, Jen Spitzer, Kelly Stage, Cassie Thomas, Amanda Thompson, Olga Valbuena, Laura Veneskey, Ania Wajnberg, Lauren Walsh, and Jessica Wolfe. My parents, Brad and Sharon, and my siblings, Derek, Katharine, and Helen, have also offered a tremendous amount of support. And thank you to my dog, Millie, who always hangs out with me while I read and write.

Editor: David Cashion
Designer: Darilyn Lowe Carnes
Production Manager: Michael Kaserkie

Library of Congress Control Number: 2017956805

ISBN: 978-1-4197-3237-9
eISBN: 978-1-68335-342-3

Text copyright © 2018 Susan Harlan
Illustrations by Becca Stadtlander

Cover © 2018 Abrams

Printed and bound in China
10 9 8 7 6 5 4 3 2 1

Abrams Image books are available at special discounts when purchased in quantity for premiums and promotions as well as fundraising or educational use. Special editions can also be created to specification. For details, contact specialsales@abramsbooks.com or the address below.

Abrams Image® is a registered trademark of Harry N. Abrams, Inc.

ABRAMS The Art of Books
195 Broadway, New York, NY 10007
abramsbooks.com